WILLIAMS
SONOMA
CALIFORNIA

JUNIOR CHEF
MASTER CLASS

PHOTOGRAPHY BY
AUBRIE PICK

weldon**owen**

CONTENTS

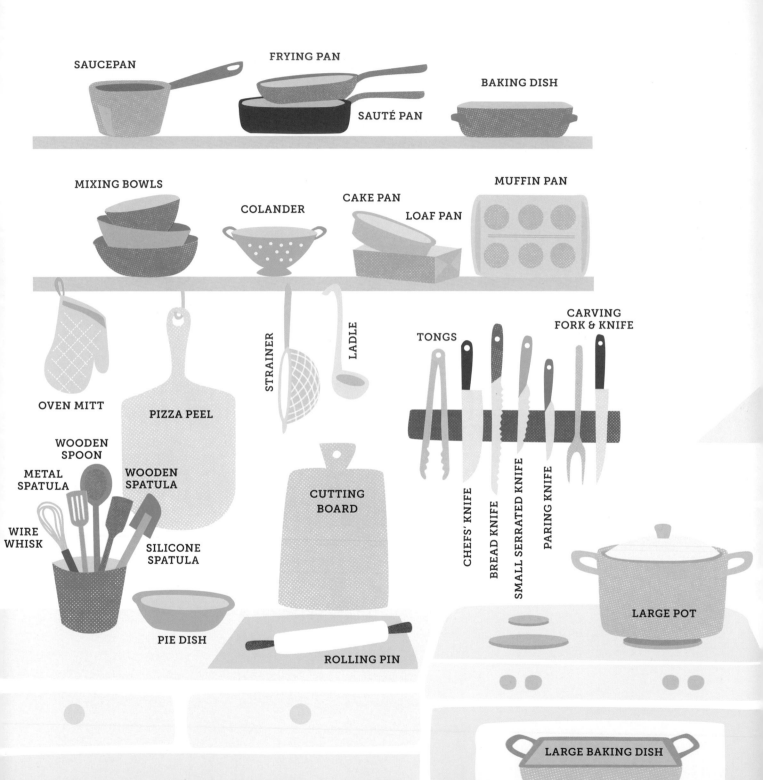

SAUCEPAN

FRYING PAN

SAUTÉ PAN

BAKING DISH

MIXING BOWLS

COLANDER

CAKE PAN

LOAF PAN

MUFFIN PAN

OVEN MITT

PIZZA PEEL

STRAINER

LADLE

TONGS

CARVING FORK & KNIFE

WOODEN SPOON

METAL SPATULA

WOODEN SPATULA

WIRE WHISK

SILICONE SPATULA

CUTTING BOARD

CHEFS' KNIFE

BREAD KNIFE

SMALL SERRATED KNIFE

PARING KNIFE

PIE DISH

ROLLING PIN

LARGE POT

LARGE BAKING DISH

GETTING READY TO COOK

ORGANIZATION

Learning to cook like a master chef is sure to be a fun and rewarding experience, but it is a talent you will likely need to perfect over time and with some effort. The first lesson every young chef needs to learn is the practice of *mise en place,* literally "everything in its place." Before you begin to cook, read through the recipe from start to finish and get out the ingredients and equipment you'll need. Prepare the ingredients in advance as much as possible and assemble them neatly around your work area for easy access. The recipes in this book will note the best tools for particular tasks, but there are a few basic tools you should try to have on hand for essential food preparation and cooking techniques.

KNIVES

Start with a basic set of knives, then add more specialty knives as you determine your cutlery needs. A **paring knife** has a small, tapered blade that is best for small-scale work such as peeling, coring, trimming, and slicing small fruits and vegetables. A **chefs' knife** has a large, tapered blade well suited to a variety of kitchen tasks, such as chopping, dicing, and slicing medium to large fruits and vegetables. A **long serrated knife**, commonly known as a bread knife, is designed to slice through thick, soft breads or cakes. A **small serrated knife** is a good tool for slicing through smaller soft fruits and vegetables, such as citrus and tomatoes. A **carving knife** has a long, narrow blade designed to easily slice through meat and maneuver around bones. Pair it with a **carving fork** to steady the item you are cutting.

POTS & PANS

Two **saucepans**, one 2 quart and one 4 quart, are best for stovetop cooking. Use a **large pot**, 6 quarts or more, for boiling water, making soup, and cooking large ingredients. A **sauté pan** has high, straight sides to help prevent food from bouncing out of the pan when it is being stirred, turned, or flipped; it usually also has a thicker bottom designed to conduct and hold heat well, and a lid for containing evaporation while cooking. A **frying pan**, also known as a skillet, is a broad pan with sides that flare outward, making it useful for cooking foods that must be stirred often or slid from the pan; it's best to have at least two frying pans, one small and one large, to use depending on the amount and size of the ingredients you are cooking.

COOKING TOOLS

Within a short reach of your cooking and preparation area should be all the simple tools you will commonly need: a **wooden spoon** or other large spoon for stirring, a **silicone spatula** for folding ingredients together, a **metal spatula** for flipping ingredients while cooking (or a wooden one for nonstick pans), a **slotted spoon** for scooping up solid ingredients while leaving liquid behind, **tongs** for turning ingredients while cooking, a **wire whisk** for quickly blending liquid ingredients, and a **strainer** for draining liquid from solid ingredients.

BASIC TECHNIQUES

INGREDIENT PREPARATION

Once your tools are assembled, it's time to ready your ingredients. Rinse fresh fruits and vegetables in water, then prepare them as requested in the recipe. Keep your hands and work area clean and put everything away as soon as you've finished using it. Also, be deliberate in everything you do, whether it's wielding a knife or tasting a salad dressing to see if it needs more salt. Your finished dishes will benefit from the extra effort.

KNIFE SKILLS

Learning how to choose, hold, and use a knife is especially important for young cooks. When selecting a knife, consider the item to be cut, then pick out a knife that is both suitable for the task and feels comfortable in your hand.

Holding a Knife

Hold the knife firmly by the handle, as if you were shaking someone's hand. Hold down the item you are cutting with your other hand, placing the flat side of the food down to keep it steady whenever you can. Curl under the fingers of the hand that's holding the food so your knuckles keep your fingertips out of harm's way. With the tip of the knife pointing down, start to cut, bringing the handle up and down and keeping the knife facing away from your body.

Chopping

Grasp the handle of a chefs' knife and, with your other hand, steady the top of the knife blade near its tip against the cutting board. Raise and lower the knife handle in a chopping motion, slowly swinging the blade back and forth across the food until the desired texture is achieved, ranging from coarsely chopped, to chopped, to finely chopped, to minced. Coarsely chopped foods are quite chunky, whereas minced foods are reduced to small bits.

Slicing

Place the food on the cutting board and steady it with your free hand, tucking your fingertips in toward your palm and keeping the side of the blade gently against your knuckles. With the knife held in your other hand, cut slices of the desired thickness.

Dicing

Cut uniform slices (working lengthwise if the item is oblong), cut the slices again to make strips, then cut across the strips to make cubes.

MEASURING

Use a set of measuring spoons (usually ¼ teaspoon, ½ teaspoon, 1 teaspoon, and 1 tablespoon) to measure small amounts of liquid and dry ingredients.

Liquids

Measure liquids in clear measuring pitchers with rulers printed on the side and a lip for pouring. Place the measuring pitcher on a flat surface, add the liquid, and check the measurement at eye level to make sure it is accurate.

Dry Ingredients

Measure dry ingredients, such as sugar or flour, by spooning the ingredient into the proper-size flat-topped measuring cup, loosely heaping it, then leveling the ingredient by running the back of a knife flush over the rim of the cup.

» HOW TO CHOP

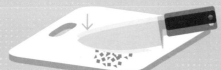

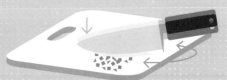

1 Grasping the handle of the knife with one hand, hold the tip of the knife against the board with the other hand.

2 Keeping the knife tip steady, raise the handle up and down in a chopping motion to cut all the pieces.

3 As you move the handle up and down, sweep the knife back and forth in a slow arc until the ingredient is chopped as desired.

» HOW TO SLICE

1 Lay the item to be cut firmly on the cutting board, first trimming a thin slice from one side if needed to rest flat.

2 Holding the item to be cut with curled fingers to keep fingertips safe, slice with the knife blade perpendicular to the cutting board.

3 Slice the food while resting the flat side of the knife blade gently against your knuckles, allowing them to guide the width of your slices.

» HOW TO DICE

1 Cut the item to be diced in half. Lay each half, cut side down, on the cuttting board.

2 Cut each half into even slices the same width as your intended dice, working lengthwise if the item is long.

3 Cut the long slices into lengthwise strips, then turn and cut crosswise into dice.

» HOW TO MEASURE

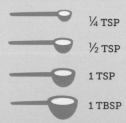

¼ TSP

½ TSP

1 TSP

1 TBSP

Check liquid measurements at eye level to ensure accuracy.

Spoon dry ingredients into a flat-topped measuring cup until mounded on top. Using the back of a knife, sweep off the excess level with the rim of the cup.

BREAKFAST

EASY EGGS BENEDICT

A good, smooth hollandaise can be a challenge for cooks, since the sauce thickens using heat that must be high enough to cook the eggs but low enough to prevent curdling them. Problem solved: Microwave heat, in 15-second bursts with lots of whisking in between, yields perfect hollandaise in under a minute.

1 MAKE THE HOLLANDAISE

Put the butter in a small microwave-safe cup or bowl; microwave on high until melted, about 30 seconds. In a microwave-safe bowl, combine the egg yolks, lemon juice, ⅛ teaspoon salt, and a few grinds of pepper. Using the technique below to steady the bowl, slowly pour in the melted butter while whisking constantly. Microwave on high, stopping to whisk vigorously every 15 seconds, until thickened slightly, about 45 seconds total. Keep warm until ready to serve.

2 POACH THE EGGS

Working in batches, poach the eggs according to the directions on page 23, setting each one aside on a paper towel-lined plate until all are cooked.

3 ASSEMBLE THE EGGS BENEDICTS

Heat a frying pan over medium heat. Add the Canadian bacon and cook, turning once, until warmed through, about 2 minutes. Toast the muffin halves until golden brown. Lightly butter the toasted muffins and place 2 halves on each plate. Top each muffin half with a slice of Canadian bacon, a warm egg, and about 2 tablespoons of the hollandaise sauce. Garnish with the parsley, if using, and serve.

FOR THE HOLLANDAISE SAUCE
½ cup unsalted butter
2 large egg yolks
2 tablespoons fresh lemon juice
Salt and freshly ground pepper

FOR THE EGGS BENEDICT
8 large eggs
8 slices Canadian bacon
4 English muffins, split
1–2 tablespoons unsalted butter, at room temperature
2 tablespoons chopped fresh flat-leaf parsley (optional)

Make a nest with a kitchen towel and nestle the bowl in the center to steady it for hands-free mixing.

NUTTY APPLE PANCAKES WITH APPLE SYRUP

These delicious pancakes are fragrant with cinnamon, nuts, and apple. For a double dose of the fruit, an easy-to-make apple syrup is the ideal topping.

1 PREPARE THE BATTER

Peel and core the apples. Using the large holes of a box grater, shred the apples. You should have about 1½ cups. In a large bowl, sift together the flour, brown sugar, baking powder, cinnamon, salt, and baking soda. In a bowl, whisk together the milk, eggs, and melted butter. Pour over the flour mixture, then add the shredded apples and pecans. Stir just until combined. Do not overmix.

2 COOK THE PANCAKES

Heat a griddle or large nonstick frying pan over medium-high heat. Lightly grease the griddle with oil or butter. For each pancake, pour about ⅓ cup of the batter onto the griddle and spread it slightly with the back of the measuring cup. Cook until golden brown on the bottom and bubbles form and break on the surface, about 1½ minutes. Flip the pancakes and cook until the other sides are golden brown, about 1 minute longer. Transfer to a plate and keep warm until all are cooked. Repeat with the remaining batter, greasing the griddle with more oil or butter as needed.

3 SERVE THE PANCAKES

Pour the warm apple syrup into a serving pitcher. Serve the pancakes piping hot, with syrup and butter for adding at the table.

2 Golden Delicious or Granny Smith apples

2¼ cups all-purpose flour

¼ cup firmly packed golden brown sugar

2 teaspoons baking powder

½ teaspoon ground cinnamon

½ teaspoon salt

¼ teaspoon baking soda

1¾ cups whole milk, plus more as needed

2 large eggs

2 tablespoons unsalted butter, melted, plus room-temperature butter for serving

¾ cup chopped pecans

Canola oil or unsalted butter for the griddle

Apple Syrup (page 125), warmed

BERRY SMASH WHOLE-GRAIN WAFFLES WITH BERRY SYRUP

To prevent the berries from burning, use the medium-low heat setting on the waffle maker and carefully wipe the grid with paper towels between batches.

1 MAKE THE SYRUP (OPTIONAL)

In a small saucepan, combine the berries and syrup. Bring to a rapid simmer over medium-high heat, then reduce the heat to medium-low and simmer, stirring occasionally, until the berries have popped and the syrup has thickened slightly, about 30 minutes.

2 PREHEAT A WAFFLE MAKER

Meanwhile, preheat a waffle maker on the medium-low setting.

3 PREPARE THE BATTER

In a bowl, whisk together the eggs, milk, and oil. In a large bowl, whisk together the all-purpose flour, whole-wheat flour, oats, brown sugar, baking powder, cinnamon, and salt. Make a well in the center of the dry ingredients, pour in the milk mixture, and whisk gently just until combined but with a few lumps. Gently stir in the berries.

4 COOK THE WAFFLES

When the waffle maker is ready, spoon batter over the cooking grid, distributing the blackberries evenly; a standard 7-inch waffle maker requires about ½ cup batter per waffle. Close the lid and cook until the steam subsides or the indicator light signals that the waffle is ready, 3–4 minutes. Carefully open the lid and transfer the waffle to a plate. Serve right away with berry syrup, if using. Repeat with the remaining batter, serving each waffle as it's ready.

FOR THE BERRY SYRUP
(OPTIONAL)

3 cups fresh or thawed frozen blackberries or blueberries

½ cup pure maple syrup

FOR THE WAFFLES

2 large eggs

1½ cups whole milk

½ cup canola oil

¾ cup all-purpose flour

½ cup whole-wheat flour

½ cup rolled oats

2 tablespoons firmly packed golden brown sugar

1 tablespoon baking powder

½ teaspoon ground cinnamon

¼ teaspoon salt

1 cup fresh or thawed frozen blackberries or blueberries

GALAXY DOUGHNUTS

These swirly doughnuts recall the starbursts and nebulas of distant solar systems. They may look tricky to prepare, but they're actually quite simple. Make sure you have an adult nearby whenever you are cooking with hot oil.

1 MAKE THE DOUGH

In a bowl, sift together the all-purpose flour, cake flour, cocoa powder, baking powder, baking soda, and salt. In a large bowl, using an electric mixer on low speed (use the paddle attachment for a stand mixer), beat the egg and sugar until creamy and pale. Add the buttermilk, melted butter, and vanilla and beat until blended. Add the flour mixture and beat, still on low speed, just until the mixture comes together into a soft dough. Cover and refrigerate the dough until firm, at least 30 minutes and up to 1 hour.

2 HEAT THE OIL

Line a baking sheet with paper towels. Pour oil into a deep-fryer or deep, heavy-bottomed sauté pan to a depth of 2 inches and warm over medium-high heat until it reads 360°F on a deep-frying thermometer.

3 CUT OUT THE DOUGHNUTS

On a generously floured work surface, roll out the dough into a circle 10 inches in diameter and ½ inch thick. Using a 3-inch round doughnut cutter, cut out as many doughnuts and holes as possible. Gather up the scraps and repeat rolling and cutting.

4 FRY THE DOUGHNUTS

Carefully lower 2–5 doughnuts and holes into the hot oil and deep-fry until dark brown and crusty on the first side, about 1½ minutes. Turn over and cook until dark brown and crusty on the second side, about 1 minute longer. Transfer to the prepared baking sheet. Repeat to fry the remaining doughnuts and holes, allowing the oil to return to 360°F between batches.

Continued on page 18 »

1 cup all-purpose flour, plus flour for dusting

1 cup cake flour

¼ cup unsweetened cocoa powder, preferably Dutch-process

1 teaspoon baking powder

½ teaspoon baking soda

½ teaspoon salt

1 large egg

½ cup sugar

½ cup buttermilk

1 tablespoon unsalted butter, melted

1 teaspoon pure vanilla extract

Canola or peanut oil for deep-frying

3 cups Vanilla Doughnut Glaze (page 125)

Pink, blue, and purple gel paste food coloring

Edible glitter and/or edible silver star sprinkles for decorating (optional)

» Continued from page 17

5 PREPARE THE GLAZE

Divide the glaze evenly between 2 bowls. Dip a toothpick into the pink food coloring, then dip the coloring into a bowl of glaze. Dip a clean toothpick into the blue food coloring, then dip the coloring into the same bowl. Do the same with another clean toothpick and the purple food coloring. Then use the toothpick to gently swirl the food colorings into the icing. Don't over-swirl or the colors will blend together. Repeat this process with the second bowl of glaze.

6 DIP THE DOUGHNUTS

Dip the top of a doughnut into the glaze and gently twist it to let any excess glaze drip off. Place the doughnut, glaze side up, on a platter and sprinkle with edible glitter and/or stars (if using). Repeat with the remaining doughnuts. When the first bowl of glaze no longer has colored swirls, or if the colors have started to blend together too much, use the other bowl of glaze. Let the glaze set for 10 minutes, then serve.

1 Dip a toothpick into pink food coloring, then into the glaze. Repeat with blue and purple coloring, then swirl.

2 Dip one side of each doughnut into the bowl of glaze, taking care not to overmix the colors.

3 Place the doughnuts, glaze side up, on a rack or a serving plate until the glaze is just set, then serve.

CLASSIC POPOVERS WITH STRAWBERRY BUTTER

The best popovers boast a dramatic rise in the oven, a golden brown crust, and moist, hollow interiors that provide the perfect medium for sweet strawberry butter. A popover pan is designed with deep cups to promote an even spread of heat and the highest puff, but a standard muffin pan will also work well.

1 MAKE THE STRAWBERRY BUTTER

In a bowl, using an electric mixer on medium speed, beat the butter, sugar, and salt until creamy. Beat in the strawberries. Transfer to a ramekin, cover with plastic wrap pressed directly on top, and refrigerate until serving.

2 MAKE THE POPOVER BATTER

Preheat the oven to 450°F. In a bowl, stir together the flour and salt. Make a well in the center of the flour mixture, add the milk and eggs, and whisk just until combined. Pour the batter into a glass measuring cup or a pitcher.

3 HEAT THE PAN

Place a 12-cup popover pan or standard muffin pan in the oven and heat until hot, about 2 minutes. Remove from the oven and spoon 1 teaspoon of the melted butter into each cup. Divide the batter evenly among the cups, filling them halfway.

4 BAKE THE POPOVERS

Bake for 10 minutes. Reduce the oven temperature to 375°F and continue to bake, without opening the oven door, until the popovers are puffed, crisp, and golden brown, 20–25 minutes longer. Using a fork, gently remove the popovers from the pan and serve piping hot with the strawberry butter.

FOR THE STRAWBERRY BUTTER

½ cup unsalted butter, at room temperature

¼ cup powdered sugar

Pinch of salt

4 large strawberries, at room temperature, chopped

FOR THE POPOVERS

1 cup all-purpose flour

½ teaspoon salt

1 cup whole milk

2 large eggs, at room temperature, beaten

4 tablespoons unsalted butter, melted

FRIED EGG SANDWICH WITH BACON, AVOCADO & TOMATO

If you approach breakfast as fuel for the day, this yummy, multilayered sandwich is the way to go. Protein? Check. Vitamins? Check. Fiber? Check. It's the whole package and it's absolutely delicious.

1 ASSEMBLE THE SANDWICH

Place 1 slice of cheese on 1 slice of bread, then layer on the bacon, egg, avocado, tomato, and second slice of cheese. Season to taste with salt and pepper, then top with the remaining bread slice, pressing firmly. Spread the butter evenly over the top and bottom bread slices.

2 COOK THE SANDWICH

Heat a frying pan over medium heat or heat a panini press if you have one. Add the sandwich to the pan and press firmly with the back of a spatula, or slip the sandwich into the press and close the top. Cook, turning once in the pan and pressing gently, until golden brown on both sides, about 4 minutes total.

3 SERVE THE SANDWICH

Transfer the sandwich to a cutting board, cut in half, and serve hot.

2 slices cheese, such as mozzarella, provolone, Monterey jack, or Cheddar

2 slices bread, such as whole-grain, sourdough, or coarse country bread

2 bacon slices, cooked and cut in half crosswise

1 Fried Egg (page 22)

¼ avocado, peeled and sliced

2–3 slices tomato, drained on paper towels

Kosher salt and freshly ground pepper

Unsalted butter for spreading

EGGS FOUR WAYS

Cooking eggs to perfection can have as much to do with personal preference as technique. Learn the best methods, then modify them to suit your taste. Most recipes in these pages call for two eggs per person, but you can vary the number to cook as many or as few as you like.

BOILED EGGS

Place the eggs in a saucepan and cover with cold water by 2 inches. Bring to a boil over medium-high heat. When the water comes to a boil, cover the pan, remove from the heat, and let the eggs stand in the water for 2 minutes for soft-boiled or up to 12 minutes for hard-boiled. Drain the eggs and rinse under cold running water until cool. When the eggs are cool, crack and peel them.

8 large eggs

FRIED EGGS

To prepare sunny-side-up eggs, in a large frying pan, preferably nonstick, heat 1 tablespoon of the olive oil or butter over medium heat. Crack 4 of the eggs into the pan. Season to taste with salt and pepper. Cook until the whites are opaque and the yolks thicken, 2–3 minutes. Transfer to plates and serve, or keep warm until all are cooked. Repeat with the remaining 1 tablespoon olive oil and eggs.

2 tablespoons olive oil or butter

8 large eggs

Salt and freshly ground pepper

To prepare over-easy, over-medium, or over-hard eggs, cook as directed above, then carefully flip the eggs with a nonstick spatula and cook for about 30 seconds longer for eggs over easy, about 1 minute longer for eggs over medium, and about 1½ minutes longer for eggs over hard.

Tip: Start with cold eggs directly from the refrigerator. The yolks are more likely to stay intact when you crack the eggs.

POACHED EGGS

Pour water into a large, deep sauté pan to a depth of 2 inches and bring to a gentle simmer over medium-low heat. One at a time, crack 4 of the eggs into a ramekin or small cup and gently slide the egg into the simmering water. Make sure they are not touching. Cook until the whites begin to set, about 2 minutes, then gently turn the eggs with a slotted spoon. Continue to cook until the whites are opaque and fully cooked and the yolks are still runny, about 2 minutes longer. Using the slotted spoon, lift each egg from the simmering water, draining well. Blot the bottom of each egg briefly on a paper towel and serve, or keep warm until all are cooked. Repeat with the remaining 4 eggs.

8 large eggs

SCRAMBLED EGGS

In a bowl, whisk the eggs with the milk and season to taste with salt and pepper. In a large nonstick frying pan, melt the butter over medium-low heat. Pour in the egg mixture and cook without stirring for 1 minute. Using a silicone spatula, gently stir the eggs, allowing the uncooked eggs to run to the bottom of the pan. Cook, stirring often, until the eggs are set but still creamy, about 4 minutes. Transfer to plates and serve.

8 large eggs

2 tablespoons whole milk

Salt and freshly ground pepper

2 tablespoons unsalted butter

CHOCOLATE BABKA

Babka is a sweet, yeasted brioche-like bread swirled with a filling of chocolate and cinnamon that hails from Eastern European Jewish traditions. This simplified version is just as delicious as the intricate original. The bread is best when warm from the oven, but it's also tasty when lightly toasted with butter.

1 ACTIVATE THE YEAST

In the bowl of a stand mixer, whisk together the milk, honey, yeast, and ¼ cup of the flour. Set aside until the yeast mixture becomes frothy, about 10 minutes.

2 MAKE THE DOUGH

Fit the stand mixer with the dough hook attachment. Add the egg, salt, and remaining 2 cups flour to the yeast mixture in the bowl. Beat on low speed until the ingredients start to come together. Increase the speed to medium and add the butter, a few tablespoons at a time, until incorporated, scraping down the sides of the bowl as needed. The dough will start out very shaggy but should become soft (but still slightly sticky) after about 4 minutes. Continue to beat on medium speed for about 5 minutes longer. Form the dough into a ball and transfer to a large, buttered bowl. Cover with plastic wrap and let rise in a warm spot until doubled, about 1½ hours.

3 MAKE THE FILLING

In the bowl of a food processor, combine the chocolate chips, cocoa, sugar, and cinnamon. Process until well combined and the chips are chopped fairly small. Add the melted butter and process to a thick paste. Set aside.

4 PREPARE THE PAN

Spray an 8½ x 4-inch or 9 x 5-inch loaf pan with cooking spray, then line it with a piece of parchment paper large enough to leave a 1- to 2-inch overhang along the longer sides.

Continued on page 25 »

FOR THE DOUGH

¾ cup whole milk, warmed (105°-110°F)

1 tablespoon honey

1 package (2¼ teaspoons) active dry yeast

2¼ cups all-purpose flour, plus flour for dusting

1 large egg, at room temperature

1 teaspoon kosher salt

½ cup unsalted butter, at room temperature, plus butter for the bowl

FOR THE FILLING

¾ cup mini semisweet chocolate chips

¼ cup unsweetened cocoa powder

¼ cup sugar

¼ teaspoon ground cinnamon

4 tablespoons unsalted butter, melted

» *Continued from page 24*

5 SHAPE THE LOAF

Transfer the dough to a lightly floured work surface and roll it out into a 10 x 12-inch rectangle, with a long edge facing you. Gently spread the chocolate filling over the dough in an even layer, taking care not to tear the dough (the filling is quite thick, so you might want to use your fingers to help spread it). Starting with the long edge closest to you, tightly roll up the dough as you would cinnamon rolls. Cut the dough log in half lengthwise. Position the two dough pieces so they form an X, then twist the ends twice on one side and then on the other. Scrunch the loaf together so it's the length of the loaf pan, then carefully transfer it to the prepared pan. Lay a piece of plastic wrap loosely over the top. Let the dough rise until doubled in size, about 1 hour.

6 BAKE THE LOAF

Preheat the oven to 375°F. When the dough has risen, remove the plastic wrap. In a small bowl, whisk together the egg and water and gently brush the egg wash over the top of the dough. Bake until golden brown, about 40 minutes. Transfer the loaf pan to a wire rack and let the babka cool in the pan for 15 minutes. Turn the babka out onto the rack and gently remove the parchment. Let cool completely, then slice and serve.

FOR THE LOAF

Cooking spray

1 large egg

1 teaspoon water

1 Cut the dough log in half lengthwise, then position the halves so they form an X.

2 Twist the ends twice on one side, then on the other, to form a chocolate-swirled loaf.

CITRUS TARTINES

Marmalade-glazed wheels of blood orange caramelize atop buttery pastry squares in these tasty tarts. Swap in any of your favorite fruits with a matching jam or jelly. Try sliced apples or peaches, fresh berries, or halved apricots.

1 PREHEAT THE OVEN

Preheat the oven to 400°F. Line a rimmed baking sheet with parchment paper.

2 PREPARE THE PASTRY

On a lightly floured work surface, gently roll out the puff pastry into a 9-inch square. Using a sharp paring knife, cut the pastry into 4 equal squares. Place the pastry squares well apart on the prepared baking sheet. Beat the egg with 1 teaspoon of the water and brush the entire surface of each square with the mixture.

3 BAKE THE TARTINES

Bake the pastry shells for 7 minutes. Remove the pan from the oven and spread 1 tablespoon of the marmalade over each shell. Arrange the orange slices in a single layer over the marmalade, trimming them to fit if necessary. In a small bowl, mix the remaining 2 tablespoons marmalade with the remaining 1 teaspoon water and brush over the oranges. Return the pan to the oven. Bake until the pastries are golden brown, about 10 minutes longer. Serve warm.

All-purpose flour for dusting

1 sheet frozen puff pastry, thawed but still very cold

1 large egg

2 teaspoons warm water

6 tablespoons orange marmalade

2 blood oranges, peeled and cut into wheels (see below)

1 Using a small, serrated knife, cut a thick slice from the top and bottom of each citrus fruit.

2 Stand each fruit upright. Following its curve, cut off the peel in thick slices.

3 Set the fruit on its side and cut crosswise into slices, discarding any seeds.

FRUITY SMOOTHIES

Learn to make the smoothies here, then experiment with your own favorite ingredients and serving ideas. Try layering different flavors, rimming glasses like party drinks, or swirling flavors together. To rim glasses like these, run an orange slice around the glass rim, then dip it in a saucer filled with toasted shredded coconut (as here) or turbinado sugar.

LAVA FLOW

In a blender, combine 1 cup ice cubes, 3 bananas, 1 cup frozen diced pineapple, 1½ cups whole milk or nut milk, and 3 tablespoons coconut cream. Blend until smooth, then divide among 3 glasses. Add 1 cup thawed frozen sweetened strawberries to the blender and blend until smooth, then divide among the glasses.

makes
3
servings

MANGO SMOOTHIE

In a blender, combine 1 cup ice cubes, 2 bananas, 4 cups fresh or thawed frozen mango cubes, ¾ cup low-fat vanilla yogurt, and 1 cup orange juice. Blend until smooth.

TROPICAL GREEN

In a blender, combine 1 cup ice cubes, 2 bananas, 3 cups frozen mangoes, 1 cup firmly packed spinach leaves, and 1 cup coconut water. Blend until smooth.

BERRY BLAST

In a blender, combine 1 cup ice cubes, 2 bananas, 4 cups frozen mixed berries, ¾ cup low-fat vanilla yogurt, ½ cup red grapes, and 1 cup coconut water. Blend until smooth.

PINEAPPLE SMOOTHIE

In a blender, combine 1 cup ice cubes, 2 bananas, 4 cups fresh or thawed frozen pineapple cubes, ¾ cup low-fat vanilla yogurt, and 1 cup orange juice. Blend until smooth.

BACON, EGG & SPINACH MUFFIN CUPS

makes
6-12
servings

Bake these easy egg cups for a healthy breakfast one day and you'll have enough left over for quick snacks throughout the week. Refrigerate the leftover cups, then reheat in the microwave. For a lighter version, use turkey bacon and swap in purchased egg whites for half the eggs.

1 PREPARE THE MUFFIN PAN

Preheat the oven to 375°F. Coat the 12 cups of a standard muffin pan with cooking spray.

2 PREPARE THE EGG MIXTURE

Rinse the frozen spinach in a colander with cold running water for 10-20 seconds, then let it thaw while you cook the bacon. In a frying pan, fry the bacon over medium heat, stirring often, until lightly browned on the edges, 3-4 minutes. Transfer the bacon to a paper towel–lined plate and pour off all but 1 tablespoon of the bacon fat in the pan. Return the pan to low heat, add the green onion, and cook, stirring, for 1 minute. Add the onion to the plate with the bacon. In a bowl, whisk the eggs and milk until blended. Squeeze the spinach dry with your hands and add to the egg mixture. Add the cheese, bacon, and green onion. Stir gently until mixed.

3 COOK THE MUFFINS

Divide the egg mixture evenly among the prepared muffin cups. Bake until the eggs are puffy and set, 20-22 minutes. Serve warm or at room temperature.

Cooking spray

¼ package (2½ oz) frozen spinach leaves or 1 cup frozen loose spinach leaves

4 bacon slices, thinly sliced crosswise

2 tablespoons thinly sliced green onion

8 large eggs

¼ cup milk

¾ cup shredded Monterey jack cheese

LEEK, POTATO & GRUYÈRE FRITTATA

To make a classic one-pan frittata, well-beaten eggs and filling ingredients are first cooked in a frying pan on the stove top, then finished in the oven. Before chopping the leek, make sure to halve it lengthwise and rinse under cold running water to remove any grit it may have picked up while growing.

1 COOK THE LEEK

In a large ovenproof frying pan, warm 1 tablespoon of the oil over medium-low heat. Add the leek and cook, stirring occasionally, until tender, about 5 minutes. Transfer to a plate and set aside.

2 COOK THE POTATOES

Add the remaining 1 tablespoon oil to the pan and return to medium-low heat. Add the sliced potatoes and use a sturdy, heatproof spatula to turn the potatoes, evenly coating them with oil. Cook, turning as needed with the spatula, until tender and lightly browned, about 15 minutes. Add the cooked leeks to the potatoes and turn gently to mix.

3 COOK THE EGG MIXTURE

Whisk together the eggs, salt, and pepper. Gently whisk in the cheese. Pour the egg mixture over the potato mixture, distributing the cheese and potatoes evenly in the pan. Cook over medium heat until the eggs begin to set at the edges, 1–2 minutes. Using the spatula, lift the cooked edge of the frittata and tilt the frying pan to allow the liquid egg on top to flow underneath. Continue cooking, occasionally lifting the frittata and tilting it again, until the top is almost set, about 4 minutes longer. Meanwhile, place a rack in the middle of the oven and preheat the broiler.

4 BROWN THE FRITTATA

Place the frittata under the broiler until the frittata puffs and turns golden brown, 1–2 minutes. Cut into wedges and serve.

2 tablespoons olive oil

½ cup chopped leek, white and pale green parts only

2 Yukon gold potatoes, thinly sliced

8 large eggs

½ teaspoon kosher salt

⅛ teaspoon freshly ground pepper

½ cup shredded Gruyère cheese

SOUPS & SALADS

WATERMELON, MANGO & AVOCADO SALAD WITH MINT & LIME

An enticing combination of colors, flavors, and textures comes together in this fruit-forward salad. You can prepare the watermelon and mango a few hours in advance, but don't cut the avocado or tear the mint until just before serving.

1 DICE THE WATERMELON

Cut the watermelon in half. Place the halves, cut sides down, on a cutting board. Using a sharp knife and following the contour of the fruit, cut away the rind, including all of the white flesh, until you are left with only the melon. Cut the watermelon halves into 1-inch slices, then lay the slices flat and cut into ½-inch cubes. Transfer to a serving platter.

2 DICE THE MANGO

Hold the mango on a narrow side on a cutting board. Using a large, sharp knife, cut just to one side of the center to cut the mango flesh from the wide flat pit. Turn the mango and cut the flesh from the other side. Using a small, sharp knife, cut off the mango peel, dice or slice the flesh, and add to the platter.

3 DICE THE AVOCADO

Using the small knife, cut into the center of the avocado, cutting all the way around the avocado when you reach the big round pit in the center. Separate the avocado halves. Use the tip of a spoon to remove the pit, then remove the peel, and dice or slice the avocado. Add the avocado to the platter.

4 ADD THE LIME

Sprinkle the lime zest and juice all over the watermelon. Toss gently with your hands to mix. Garnish with the nuts and mint, and serve.

1 small seedless watermelon, about 3 lb (about 3 cups cubed watermelon)

1 ripe mango

1 avocado

Grated zest and juice of 1 lime

¼ cup chopped pistachios or toasted sliced almonds

6 fresh mint leaves, torn into small pieces

» FRESH LIME JUICE
adds bright flavor to this
fruity mix and helps
prevent the avocado and
mango from browning.

MIXED CITRUS SALAD WITH CELERY CURLS

Mâche is a mild, tender green that even the pickiest salad eaters will love. Serve it with your favorite citrus, which is at its best during the winter months. Try a mix of navel oranges, blood oranges, tangerines, mandarins, and pomelos for the prettiest, tastiest salad.

1 MAKE THE CELERY CURLS

Cut the celery ribs in half lengthwise. Using a serrated vegetable peeler or a mandoline, shave the celery lengthwise into thin strips. Cut the strips in half crosswise and place in a bowl of cold water. Set aside.

2 CUT THE CITRUS

Separate the mâche leaves and put them in a shallow serving bowl. Cut the citrus into wheels (see page 27), reserving the juices for the vinaigrette. Transfer the slices to the bowl with the mâche. Using a serrated knife, cut each kumquat crosswise into very thin slices, discarding any seeds. Scatter the kumquat slices over the salad.

3 ADD THE CELERY AND JICAMA

Drain the celery and distribute it evenly over the salad, along with the jicama. Scatter the almonds and blossoms (if using) over the top.

4 MIX THE SALAD

Pour the reserved citrus juices into a glass measuring cup. Add enough additional orange juice to measure ½ cup, then add the vinegar. Whisking constantly, slowly add the olive oil and whisk until well combined. Season to taste with salt and pepper. Drizzle the vinaigrette over the salad, toss gently to coat, and serve.

FOR THE SALAD

2 ribs celery

2 bunches mâche or 2 cups mixed greens

2 lb mixed citrus fruits

8 kumquats

1 cup peeled, diced jicama

¼ cup sliced almonds, toasted

¼ cup edible blossoms (optional)

FOR THE VINAIGRETTE

Fresh orange juice, as needed

1 tablespoon white wine vinegar or champagne vinegar

¼ cup extra-virgin olive oil

Salt and freshly ground pepper

GREEN & YELLOW CHOPPED SALAD WITH CREAMY LEMON VINAIGRETTE

This crisp chopped salad provides the perfect dish for honing your chopping skills. For an easy shortcut, use a food processor with a julienne blade, a mandoline, or a spiralizer for the zucchini, yellow squash, and beets. Swap out any ingredient for another of your favorites—try matchsticks of peeled jicama and 1-inch pieces of raw green bean.

1 PREPARE THE VEGETABLES

Using a sharp knife, mandoline, spiralizer, or food processor fitted with a julienne blade, cut the zucchini, squash, and beet into matchstick-size pieces. (With all tools except for the food processor, cut the squashes around the seedy core, which is best discarded.) Transfer the vegetables to a bowl and add the snow peas, bell pepper, and watercress.

2 TOSS WITH THE DRESSING

In a small jar with a lid, combine the oil, mayonnaise, lemon juice, and vinegar. Shake until blended, then season to taste with salt, pepper, and sugar. Drizzle the dressing over the salad, toss to mix, and serve.

FOR THE SALAD

1 zucchini

1 yellow crookneck squash

1 golden beet, peeled

¼ lb snow peas, cut crosswise into 1-inch pieces

1 yellow bell pepper, seeded and thinly sliced

1 bunch watercress leaves, well rinsed

FOR THE CREAMY LEMON VINAIGRETTE

¼ cup grapeseed oil or light olive oil

2 tablespoons mayonnaise or plain Greek yogurt

2 tablespoons fresh lemon juice

1 tablespoon white wine vinegar

Salt and freshly ground pepper

Pinch of sugar

» ACCORDIAN-STYLE combos like these are best achieved if the ingredients—here, a ball of fresh mozzarella and whole tomatoes—are about the same size.

CAPRESE BOMBS WITH PESTO DRESSING

If you really like the combination of tomato and mozzarella, you may just be able to finish off one of these hefty packages on your own. Or, cut the tomatoes in half just before serving.

1 CUT THE MOZZARELLA
Cut the ball of mozzarella in half lengthwise, then cut each half crosswise into 7 or 8 equal slices. Set aside.

2 CUT THE TOMATOES
Using a sharp knife, cut around the stem of each tomato to remove the core, and discard. Place the tomatoes, cut sides down, on a cutting board. Make 5 evenly spaced cuts into the smooth bottom of each tomato without cutting all the way through.

3 MAKE THE BOMBS
Insert a slice of mozzarella into each cut, aligning it as much as possible with the sides of the tomato. Place each mozzarella-stuffed tomato on a plate.

4 MAKE THE PESTO DRESSING
In a bowl, whisk together the pesto and vinegar. Add the oil in a thin stream, whisking constantly until the dressing is well blended.

5 SERVE THE BOMBS
Drizzle the dressing over the cheese-stuffed tomatoes. Season to taste with salt and pepper, and serve.

FOR THE CAPRESE BOMBS
1 ball (8 oz) fresh mozzarella
3 tomatoes (about 1½ lb)

FOR THE PESTO DRESSING
3 tablespoons Fresh Basil Pesto (page 124) or store-bought pesto
1½ tablespoons red wine vinegar
¼ cup extra-virgin olive oil
Salt and freshly ground pepper

ASIAN CHICKEN SALAD WITH PEANUT DRESSING

With its peanutty dressing, tender shredded chicken, and mix of herbs and greens, this tasty salad is a definite people pleaser. If you plan to tote it in your lunch box, pack the dressing in a separate container and toss it with the salad just before you eat.

1 MAKE THE DRESSING

In a jar with a lid, combine all the dressing ingredients. Cover and shake until evenly blended. Set aside.

2 MIX THE SALAD

Cut the core ends from the baby romaine, then thinly slice the heads crosswise. (You should have about 6 cups.) Transfer the cut romaine to a serving bowl, separating the pieces with your fingers. Add the cilantro and mint and toss to mix. Scatter the chicken over the top.

3 SERVE THE SALAD

Drizzle half of the dressing evenly over the salad and toss until evenly coated. Sprinkle with the peanuts and green onion (if using). Serve, offering the remaining dressing at the table to add if desired.

FOR THE PEANUT DRESSING

¼ cup natural peanut butter

¼ cup rice vinegar

¼ cup peanut oil

2 tablespoons water

2 tablespoons golden brown sugar

1 tablespoon toasted sesame oil

1 teaspoon tamari or soy sauce

½ teaspoon salt

FOR THE SALAD

2 heads baby romaine

¼ cup loosely packed finely chopped fresh cilantro

2 tablespoons finely chopped fresh mint

1⅓ cups shredded cooked chicken, store-bought or homemade (page 122)

½ cup chopped unsalted peanuts

1 tablespoon thinly sliced green onion (optional)

SUPERFOOD KALE & QUINOA SALAD WITH POMEGRANATE

A healthy mix of kale and quinoa provides an excellent protein- and fiber-rich building block for any superfood blend. Pomegranate seeds make a vibrant and crunchy addition. To easily extract the seeds from a pomegranate without making a mess, follow the simple directions below.

1 MAKE THE VINAIGRETTE
In a jar with a lid, combine the lemon juice, vinegar, and oil. Cover and shake until evenly blended. Taste and season with salt and pepper.

2 MIX THE SALAD
In a bowl, toss together the kale, quinoa, carrots, pomegranate seeds, mint, almonds, and sesame seeds. Just before serving, add the avocado and vinaigrette and toss gently to mix.

FOR THE LEMON VINAIGRETTE
2 tablespoons fresh lemon juice
1 tablespoon white wine vinegar
¼ cup olive oil
Salt and freshly ground pepper

FOR THE SALAD
2 cups baby kale
1 cup Steamed Quinoa (page 123)
2 small carrots, thinly sliced
¼ cup pomegranate seeds
2 tablespoons fresh mint leaves
2 tablespoons toasted sliced almonds or roasted pepitas
1 tablespoon sesame seeds
¼ avocado, peeled and sliced

1 Score the skin of a pomegranate with a knife.

2 Hold the pomegranate in water and pull the sections apart, letting the seeds sink to the bottom.

3 The skin will float. Scoop it out, then drain the seeds.

BROCCOLI & CHEDDAR SOUP WITH DICED HAM

Small chunks of salty diced ham are a last-minute addition to this cheesy soup. Skip the ham for a vegetarian rendition, or swap it for the same amount of crumbled cooked bacon or sausage.

1 PREPARE THE BROCCOLI

Using a vegetable peeler, remove the outer layer of the tough broccoli stems. Coarsely chop the broccoli florets and stems.

2 HEAT THE BROTH

In a medium saucepan over high heat, bring the broth to a boil. Reduce the heat to medium-low to maintain a gentle simmer.

3 COOK THE VEGETABLES

In a large saucepan over medium heat, melt the butter. Add the onion and cook, stirring often, until soft, about 8 minutes. Sprinkle in the flour and cook, stirring often, for 1 minute longer. Add the heated broth, chopped broccoli, lemon juice, and thyme and bring to a boil over high heat. Reduce the heat to low, cover, and simmer until the broccoli is tender, about 20 minutes. Remove the pan from the heat and let cool to lukewarm.

4 PURÉE THE VEGETABLES

Working in batches, transfer the vegetables to a food processor or blender and process until smooth, then return the soup to the saucepan. (Alternatively, use an immersion blender to purée the soup in the saucepan.) Stir in the milk and ham, and bring to a gentle simmer over low heat. Sprinkle half of the cheese into the soup and stir until melted. Season to taste with salt and pepper. If needed, add more broth to reach the desired consistency. Ladle the soup into bowls, top with the remaining cheese, and serve.

1½ lb broccoli

5 cups chicken broth, or as needed

2 tablespoons unsalted butter

1 yellow onion, finely chopped

¼ cup all-purpose flour

1 tablespoon fresh lemon juice

½ teaspoon dried thyme

2 cups whole milk

4 oz boneless ham steak, diced

8 oz sharp Cheddar cheese, shredded

Salt and freshly ground pepper

SUMMER VEGETABLE SOUP WITH CROUTONS & BASIL DRIZZLE

Roasting the vegetables before puréeing them contributes a rich depth of flavor to this vegetarian soup. A sprinkling of buttery croutons and a swirl of basil oil just before serving gives the soup an exceptionally tasty final flourish.

1 ROAST THE VEGETABLES

Preheat the oven to 425°F. In a large, heavy roasting pan, combine the leeks, carrots, zucchini, eggplants, tomatoes, and potatoes. Add ½ cup of the broth and the olive oil, season to taste with salt and pepper, and mix until the vegetables are well coated. Roast, turning once, until the vegetables are softened, about 40 minutes. Remove from the oven and let cool slightly.

2 PURÉE THE VEGETABLES

Working in batches, transfer the vegetables to a food processor or blender, adding ½ cup broth per batch, and process until the vegetables are puréed. Transfer to a large saucepan and stir in the remaining broth, the basil, and the lemon juice. (Alternatively, transfer the roasted vegetables to a large saucepan, add the broth, and use an immersion blender to purée the vegetables.) If needed, add more broth to reach the desired consistency.

3 SERVE THE SOUP

Cook over low heat for 3 minutes to blend the flavors. Season to taste with salt and pepper. Ladle the soup into individual bowls and garnish each with some croutons and a drizzle of basil oil.

2 leeks, white and pale green parts only, finely chopped

4 carrots, peeled and cut into 2-inch pieces

2 zucchini, cut into 2-inch pieces

2 Asian eggplants, cut into 2-inch pieces

2 large tomatoes, quartered

2 potatoes (about 10 oz total), peeled and cut into 2-inch pieces

4½ cups chicken broth, plus more as needed

2 tablespoons olive oil

Salt and freshly ground pepper

2 tablespoons finely chopped fresh basil

2 tablespoons fresh lemon juice

1 cup Croutons (page 122)

Basil oil for drizzling

» MISO, the thick fermented soybean paste of Japan, imparts a deep, rich flavor. High heat can damage its delicate nuance, so keep the heat low after adding it.

MISO SOUP WITH SOBA NOODLES, TOFU & MUSHROOMS

Miso soup begins with a light Japanese broth known as dashi. To make it, you need kombu (kelp) and bonito flakes (dried and smoked skipjack tuna that is shaved into thin flakes), both of which are available in Asian markets.

1 PREPARE THE TOFU

Drain the tofu and slice in half crosswise. Place both pieces of tofu on a plate and top with a second plate. Weigh down the top plate with a heavy can. Let stand for 20 minutes to drain the tofu. Pour off any water from the plate. Cut the tofu into tiny cubes. Set aside.

2 BOIL THE NOODLES

Meanwhile, bring a pot of salted water to a boil over high heat. Add the soba noodles and cook, stirring occasionally, until al dente, about 6 minutes. Add the mushrooms and carrot during the last 30 seconds of cooking. Drain, rinse under cold water, and drain again. Leave the noodles and vegetables in the strainer and set aside.

3 MAKE THE DASHI

Combine 3 cups cold water and the kombu in a saucepan. Bring to a boil over medium heat, then remove and discard the kombu. Turn off the heat, add the bonito flakes, and stir gently once. Cover and let stand for 5 minutes. Strain the soup through a fine-mesh sieve and return the broth to the saucepan. Add the noodles, sliced vegetables, and tofu and rewarm over low heat.

4 ADD THE MISO

Transfer ¼ cup of the warm broth to a small bowl, add the miso paste, and stir until smooth. Add the miso mixture to the saucepan and warm gently; do not boil. Divide the noodles, tofu, and vegetables evenly among 4 small soup bowls, then pour in the broth, dividing it evenly. Sprinkle with the green onion and serve.

2 oz firm tofu

4 oz dried soba noodles

2 oz small white mushrooms, thinly sliced

1 small carrot, peeled and thinly sliced

1 piece kombu, about 4 inches

½ cup bonito flakes

¼ cup white miso paste

1 small green onion, thinly sliced

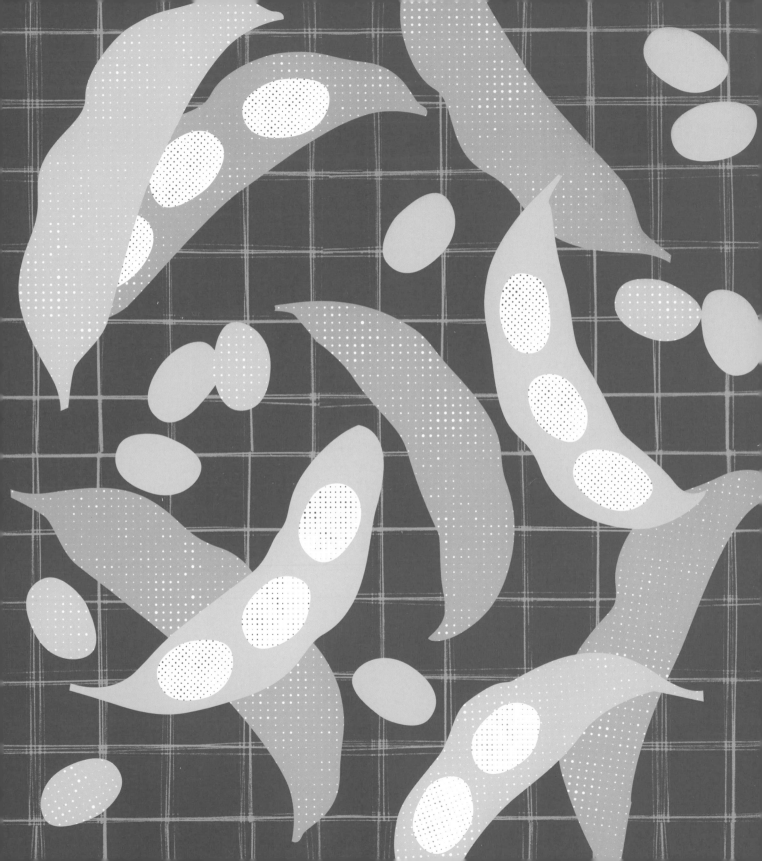

SNACKS

TEMPURA GREEN BEANS WITH SOY DIP

These veggie "fries" are so much better for you than the traditional kind, but they taste just as delicious. Serve the warm beans with the soy dip, or mix a few shots of Sriracha into a bowl of mayonnaise for a zesty mayo dip. Always take care when cooking with hot oil and ask an adult for help, if needed.

1 MAKE THE DIP

In a bowl, mix together the water, soy sauce, and mirin. Set aside.

2 MIX THE BATTER

In a large bowl, whisk together the ice water and egg. Whisk in the flour; the batter should be quite lumpy. Add the ice cubes.

3 HEAT THE OIL

Line a large plate with paper towels and set the plate near the stove. Pour oil into a heavy-bottomed saucepan or deep-fryer to a depth of 2 inches. Set the pan over medium heat and warm the oil until it reaches 360°F on a deep-frying thermometer.

4 FRY THE BEANS

Meanwhile, spread the beans out on a baking sheet and dust with about 2 tablespoons flour. When the oil is ready, submerge about one-third of the beans in the batter. Use tongs to remove them from the batter, 2 or 3 at a time, letting the excess batter drip back into the bowl, and carefully lower them into the hot oil. Fry, stirring occasionally, until crisp, about 3 minutes. Using the tongs, remove the beans from the pot. Drain them on the paper towel–lined plate and sprinkle with salt. Cook the rest of the beans in the same way, allowing the oil to return to 360°F between batches.

5 SERVE THE BEANS

Serve the fried beans alongside the bowl of soy dip.

FOR THE SOY DIP

1 cup water

⅓ cup soy sauce

⅓ cup mirin

FOR THE GREEN BEANS

1 cup ice water

1 large egg, beaten

¾ cup sifted all-purpose flour, plus flour for dusting

2 or 3 ice cubes

Vegetable oil for frying

1 lb green beans, trimmed

Salt

NO-BAKE ENERGY BALLS

Loaded with nuts, oats, and dried fruits, these nutrition-packed bites are real food that will stave off hunger for hours. Enjoy them plain, or toss the sticky-sweet balls in a bowl of sweetened cocoa powder for a truffle-like finish, if you like.

1 PROCESS THE INGREDIENTS
In a food processor or blender, combine the apples, dates, vanilla, and zest; pulse until the mixture is well chopped and forms a ball, about 30 short pulses. Add the nuts, oats, pepitas, cinnamon, and salt and process until the nuts are finely ground and the mixture forms moist clumps when pressed together with your fingers, about 2 minutes.

2 MIX THE BATTER
Roll the mixture between your palms into ¾-inch balls. Store in an airtight container in the refrigerator for up to 1 month.

¾ cup lightly packed chopped dried apples

½ cup pitted Medjool dates

1 teaspoon pure vanilla extract

1 teaspoon grated orange or lemon zest

1 cup lightly toasted nuts, such as walnuts or blanched almonds

¼ cup old-fashioned rolled oats

1 tablespoon pepitas or sesame seeds

1½ teaspoons ground cinnamon

¼ teaspoon salt

EASY CHEESY PULL-APART BREAD

All you need for this quick party snack is a loaf of good-quality bread, a trio of easy-to-source ingredients, and a hot oven. If using sun-dried tomatoes, use the oil from the jar for drizzling the loaf just before baking.

1 CUT THE LOAF

Preheat the oven to 350°F. Using a long serrated knife, cut slits in the bread about 1 inch apart, being careful to not cut all the way through and leaving about ½ inch intact on the bottom. Rotate the bread and cut slits in the opposite direction, again 1 inch apart.

2 ADD THE FILLING

In a bowl, stir together the cheese, sun-dried tomatoes, and parsley. Using your hands, stuff the cheese mixture between the cuts, working in both directions. Place the loaf on a rimmed baking sheet and drizzle the butter all over the top.

3 BAKE THE BREAD

Cover the loaf loosely with aluminum foil and bake for 15 minutes. Remove the foil and continue to bake until the cheese is melted and the top of the bread is golden brown, about 10 minutes longer. Transfer to a platter and serve.

1 round loaf artisanal bread

2 cups shredded Gruyère or mozzarella cheese

⅔ cup diced, drained sun-dried tomatoes in olive oil or chopped pitted Kalamata olives

⅓ cup loosely packed fresh parsley leaves, chopped

4 tablespoons olive oil or melted unsalted butter

1 Slice the bread at even intervals without cutting all the way through.

2 Turn and cut again at even intervals to make a grid.

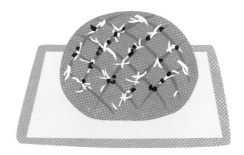

3 Stuff the filling into the cuts, drizzle with oil, and bake.

LOADED HUMMUS

Arrange a chunky garnish over one side of this favorite dip. Serve with pita chips for scooping up the hummus either plain or loaded with toppings.

1 MAKE THE HUMMUS

In a food processor, combine the chickpeas and garlic and process until the garlic is finely minced. Using a spatula, scrape down the sides of the bowl. Add the tahini, water, ¼ cup olive oil, lemon juice, and salt. Purée until the ingredients are combined but the mixture is still somewhat coarse. Transfer the hummus to a wide serving bowl and drizzle with 1 tablespoon oil.

2 LOAD THE BOWL

Scatter your choice of garnishes over one side of the hummus. Serve with pita chips.

1 can (15 oz) chickpeas, rinsed and drained

2 cloves garlic

⅓ cup tahini

¼ cup water

¼ cup plus 1 tablespoon extra-virgin olive oil

2½ tablespoons fresh lemon juice

½ teaspoon salt

1½ teaspoons finely chopped fresh flat-leaf parsley

Cherry tomatoes, carrot slices, radish slices, olive tapenade, pumpkin seeds, and/or crumbled feta for garnish

Pita chips for dipping

RANCH DIP

Ranch dip originated as a salad dressing at a dude ranch in Santa Barbara, California in 1954 and remains one of the most popular dips today.

1 MIX THE DIP

In a bowl, combine the mayonnaise, buttermilk, parsley, shallot, garlic, ½ teaspoon salt, and ¼ teaspoon pepper. Stir until blended. Taste and adjust the seasonings, if needed. Serve cold or at room temperature with your favorite dippers. Store any leftover dip in an airtight container in the refrigerator for up to 3 days.

½ cup *each* mayonnaise and buttermilk

1 tablespoon minced fresh flat-leaf parsley or 1 teaspoon dried parsley

1 teaspoon minced shallot or ½ teaspoon onion powder

1 clove garlic, minced, or ½ teaspoon garlic powder

Salt and freshly ground pepper

GREEN GODDESS DIP

Green Goddess dressing was created in San Francisco's Palace Hotel in 1923 for a special salad to honor the opening of a new play by the same name.

1 MIX THE DIP

In a food processor or blender, combine the yogurt, watercress, dill, green onion, sugar, salt, and hot-pepper sauce and process until smooth. Pour the dressing into a container with a tight-fitting lid and refrigerate for several hours or up to overnight. The dressing will be thin when first made, but it will thicken, and the flavors will mellow, when refrigerated. Shake or stir well before serving. Serve cold or at room temperature with your favorite dippers. Store any leftover dip in an airtight container in the refrigerator for up to 3 days.

1 cup plain low-fat yogurt

1 cup loosely packed watercress leaves and tender stems

2 tablespoons chopped fresh dill

1 green onion, thinly sliced

½ teaspoon sugar

½ teaspoon salt

⅛ teaspoon hot-pepper sauce

SWEET POTATO OVEN FRIES

Although known as "fries," these crispy sweet potato batons are actually oven-baked with no loss to taste or texture. Garlic and parsley adds extra flavor, but you can leave them plain, if you like. Take care when cutting sweet potatoes and always have an adult nearby for help when you need it.

1 **CUT THE POTATOES**

Preheat an oven to 450°F (220°C). Rinse and dry the sweet potatoes, but do not peel them. Cut the sweet potatoes lengthwise into slices ½ inch thick, then cut each slice into batons about ¼ inch wide and 3 inches long.

2 **BAKE THE "FRIES"**

Arrange in a single layer on a large rimmed baking sheet and toss with olive oil and ¼ teaspoon salt. Roast, stirring halfway the baking time, until tender and browned on the edges, 20 – 25 minutes.

3 **COAT WITH GARLIC**

In a large bowl, stir together the parsley and garlic. Add the warm fries to the bowl and mix gently to coat. Season to taste with more salt, if needed, and serve.

2 lb sweet potatoes

2 tablespoons olive oil

Coarse sea salt

2 tablespoons chopped fresh flat-leaf parsley leaves

1 garlic clove, minced

TASTY TOASTS

A yummy toast starts with good-quality bread. A generous slice cut from a country loaf is an excellent choice, but you can also try pugliese, ciabatta, or sourdough. Load up the toast with your favorite toppings, selecting fruity ones if you have a sweet tooth or veggies if you prefer savory. These ideas are designed for one, but you can add to the ingredients to serve more.

MOZZARELLA, SUN-DRIED TOMATO PESTO & PROSCIUTTO Spread 1 tablespoon sun-dried tomato pesto over the toast. Top with 2 slices (about 1 oz) fresh mozzarella and 1 oz thinly sliced prosciutto, distributing them evenly. Sprinkle with fresh thyme leaves. Season to taste with salt and pepper.

STRAWBERRY, BASIL, RICOTTA & HONEY Hull and slice 3 strawberries. Spread 1 tablespoon whole-milk ricotta cheese over the toast, then arrange the strawberry slices on top. Sprinkle with 1 tablespoon small basil leaves, then drizzle with 1 teaspoon honey.

PEAR, BRIE & HONEYED PINE NUTS In a small frying pan, combine 1 tablespoon pine nuts and 1 teaspoon honey. Cook, stirring, over medium heat until the nuts are golden and coated with honey, about 3 minutes. Arrange in a single layer on a plate or piece of parchment paper and let cool. Slice ½ ripe pear. Spread 1 oz sliced brie over the toast, then fan the pear slices on top. Sprinkle evenly with the pine nuts.

AVOCADO, CHERRY TOMATO & EVERYTHING BAGEL SEASONING Using a paring knife, make a lengthwise cut into the center of 1 avocado until you reach the pit, then cut all the way around the pit. Twist the avocado halves in opposite directions to separate them; set the half with the pit aside for another use. Using a spoon, scoop the flesh from the remaining half and place, cut side down, on the toast. Cut the avocado into slices on the toast, then tilt the slices to fan them out slightly. Scatter a scant ¼ cup halved cherry tomatoes over the avocado, then sprinkle with ⅛ teaspoon everything bagel seasoning or a mix of sesame seeds, sea salt, dried minced garlic and onion, and poppy seeds.

CHEWY FRUIT & NUT BARS

These homemade bars make great snacks or lunch box treats. You can assemble them in minutes and walk away while they firm up in the refrigerator—no baking required! Use this recipe as a template for variations featuring any of your favorite dried fruits and nuts.

1 PREPARE THE PAN

Line an 8-inch square baking pan with aluminum foil, leaving an inch or so of overhang on 2 opposite edges to use later as handles. Grease the foil with butter.

2 MIX THE FRUIT & NUTS

In a large bowl, stir together the brown rice cereal, almonds, cashews, cranberries, and apricots. Set aside. In a saucepan, stir or whisk together the brown rice syrup, almond butter, brown sugar, the 2 tablespoons butter, and the salt over medium heat until the mixture is smooth. Bring to a simmer and cook for 1 minute, stirring constantly to prevent scorching. Immediately pour the hot almond-butter mixture over the cereal mixture in the bowl. Using a wooden spoon, mix until the cereal, fruit, and nuts are evenly coated and distributed.

3 CUT THE BARS

With lightly buttered hands, press the mixture firmly and evenly into the prepared pan. Refrigerate until set, about 1 hour. Use the foil overhang as handles to lift the bars out of the pan and transfer to a cutting board. Using a sharp buttered knife, cut into 20 bars; remove from the foil. Layer the bars in an airtight container, with sheets of parchment or waxed paper between layers, and store in the refrigerator for up to 1 week.

2 tablespoons unsalted butter, plus butter for greasing

1½ cups puffed brown rice cereal

1 cup whole almonds

½ cup whole cashews

1 cup dried cranberries

½ cup dried apricots

½ cup brown rice syrup

¼ cup unsalted creamy almond butter

2 tablespoons firmly packed golden brown sugar

¼ teaspoon salt

TAMARI-GLAZED EDAMAME

No fussy shelling required with these savory-sweet tamari-glazed edamame pods. Simply insert a whole flavorful pod in your mouth and suck out the tender beans inside. Toss the edamame with the tamari mixture while they're still warm from cooking to readily absorb the sauce.

1 **COOK THE EDAMAME**
Cook the edamame according to the package directions.

2 **MAKE THE SAUCE**
Meanwhile, warm the oil in a small frying pan over medium-low heat. Add the garlic and ginger and cook, stirring to prevent burning, until softened, 1–2 minutes. Stir in the tamari, water, brown sugar, and vinegar and cook, stirring, over medium heat until reduced slightly, about 1 minute. Remove from the heat.

3 **SERVE THE EDAMAME**
When the edamame is ready, drain it and transfer it to the frying pan. Toss well to coat evenly. Sprinkle with the red pepper flakes and/or sesame seeds and serve.

1 package (12 oz) frozen edamame in the shell (about 4 cups)

1 teaspoon canola oil

1 small clove garlic, minced

1-inch knob fresh ginger, peeled and minced

2 tablespoons tamari or reduced-sodium soy sauce

2 tablespoons water

1½ tablespoons golden brown sugar

1 tablespoon rice vinegar

½ teaspoon red pepper flakes and/or toasted sesame seeds

MAINS

GRILLED CHICKEN SHAWARMA FLATBREAD WRAPS WITH TZATZIKI

Shawarma, a Middle Eastern specialty, is seasoned meat that is slow-roasted on a spit and sliced thin for serving. You can make a version of shawarma at home by grilling strips of marinated chicken in a grill pan, then serving them in pita bread.

1 MARINATE THE CHICKEN

In a large bowl, stir together 1 tablespoon of the olive oil, the curry powder, cumin, garlic, lemon juice, 1 teaspoon salt, and ¼ teaspoon pepper. Add the chicken and toss until well coated. Let stand at room temperature for 20 minutes.

2 PREPARE THE ONION

Meanwhile, in a small bowl, drizzle the onion with the remaining 1 tablespoon olive oil, sprinkle with salt and pepper, and toss to coat.

3 GRILL THE CHICKEN

Set a large nonstick grill pan over medium-high heat and let heat for 2 minutes. Add the onion, spreading it in an even layer, and cook, turning occasionally with tongs, until nicely browned on both sides, about 6 minutes total. Transfer to a plate and cover to keep warm. Add half of the chicken strips to the pan, spreading them in an even layer, and cook, turning once, until lightly browned on both sides and opaque throughout, about 3 minutes per side. Transfer the chicken to a plate and cover to keep warm. Repeat to cook the remaining chicken, then transfer to the plate with the first batch.

4 MAKE THE WRAPS

Carefully open the pita halves to create pockets. Fill each pocket with lettuce pieces, tomato slices, grilled onion, and grilled chicken, evenly dividing the fillings. Generously drizzle the fillings in each pita with some of the tzatziki and serve with the remaining tzatziki for adding at the table.

2 tablespoons olive oil

2 teaspoons curry powder

1 teaspoon ground cumin

2 cloves garlic, minced

Juice of ½ lemon

Salt and freshly ground pepper

4 boneless, skinless chicken breast halves, cut crosswise into ½-inch-thick strips

1 red onion, halved through the core, then cut crosswise into ¼-inch slices

3 pita breads, halved

6–8 romaine lettuce leaves, torn to fit inside pitas

2 ripe plum tomatoes, thinly sliced, or 1 cup yellow pear tomatoes, halved

2 cups Tzatziki (page 124)

CREAMY PARMESAN RISOTTO

In Italy, short-grain rice varieties, such as Arborio, Vialone Nano, and Carnaroli, are grown specifically for making risotto. You can prepare the risotto partially in advance and finish the cooking 15 minutes before serving.

1 HEAT THE BROTH

Put the broth in a saucepan and warm over low heat. Have a ladle ready for scooping the broth.

2 COOK THE RICE

In a deep saucepan, melt 2 tablespoons of the butter over low heat. Add the shallot and cook, stirring often, until translucent, about 2 minutes. Stir in the rice, coating it with the butter. Cook, stirring, until the edges of the grains are translucent, about 2 minutes.

3 STIR IN THE BROTH

Increase the heat to medium. Add 1 cup of the warm broth and simmer, stirring often, until the rice absorbs most of the broth with only a little visible liquid remaining, 5–6 minutes. Add another 1 cup broth and continue to simmer gently, stirring often, until the rice again absorbs most of the liquid, 5–6 minutes longer. (At this point, the risotto can be removed from the heat and set aside for up to 2 hours.) Stir in the remaining 1 cup broth and simmer, stirring often, until the rice absorbs most of the broth, 4–5 minutes longer. Stir in the cheese and remaining 1 tablespoon butter and season to taste with salt, white pepper, and nutmeg. The risotto should be al dente. If it is too moist, simmer for a few minutes longer; if it is too dry, stir in a little additional broth.

4 SERVE THE RISOTTO

Remove the pan from the heat when there is a little more liquid than desired, as the rice will continue to absorb it. Mound the risotto in warmed shallow bowls and serve hot.

3 cups beef, chicken, or vegetable broth, plus more as needed

3 tablespoons unsalted butter

2 tablespoons minced shallot

1 cup Arborio or Carnaroli rice

¼ cup freshly grated Parmesan cheese

Salt and ground white pepper

Freshly grated nutmeg

HOW TO MAKE PARMESAN RISOTTO

1

In a saucepan over low heat, cook the shallot in butter until translucent.

2

Add the rice and cook, stirring, until the edges of the grains are translucent.

3

Ladle hot broth into the rice mixture and cook, stirring almost continuously.

4

As the rice is stirred, the grains will gradually absorb the broth.

5

When little liquid remains, stir in more hot broth. Cook, stirring, until absorbed, then add another ladleful of broth.

6

When the grains are al dente and most of the broth has been absorbed, stir in the Parmesan and butter, then serve.

HOLIDAY TURKEY WITH GRAVY

A whole roast turkey is not difficult to achieve, nor is a perfect pan gravy when you follow the step-by-step directions (page 68). Take care when making the gravy—the roasting pan can be cumbersome to handle and the juices will be hot.

1 PREPARE THE TURKEY

Position a rack in the lower third of the oven and preheat to 325°F. Rinse the turkey inside and out and pat dry with paper towels. Trim off and discard any excess fat. Fold the wing tips underneath the back of the turkey to prevent them from overbrowning. Season inside and out with salt and pepper. Using kitchen string, tie the legs together at the ankles. Place the turkey, breast side up, on a V-shaped rack in a roasting pan. Spread 2 tablespoons of the butter over the turkey breast.

2 ROAST THE TURKEY

In a small saucepan, melt the remaining 4 tablespoons butter over low heat, then stir in the lemon zest and water. Place the roasting pan in the oven and roast the turkey, using a bulb baster to baste the turkey with the butter mixture every 20 minutes, until pan drippings have accumulated, then baste with the drippings. After 1¼ hours, add the quartered onion and carrots to the pan, stirring to coat them with the drippings. Continue to roast, basting every 30 minutes, until an instant-read thermometer inserted into the thickest part of the thigh away from the bone registers 175°F, about 1¾ hours longer (for a total roasting time of about 3 hours); cover the breast loosely with aluminum foil if it begins to overbrown during roasting.

3 MAKE THE GRAVY

Transfer the turkey to a platter and cover loosely with aluminum foil while you make the gravy. (Follow the directions on page 68.)

4 CARVE THE TURKEY

Carve the turkey at the table and serve with the gravy.

1 whole turkey (12-14 lb), at room temperature

Salt and freshly ground pepper

6 tablespoons unsalted butter, at room temperature

1 tablespoon grated lemon zest

¼ cup water

1 onion, cut into quarters

2 carrots, unpeeled, cut into 1-inch pieces

HOW TO MAKE TURKEY GRAVY

1
Using a slotted spoon, transfer the vegetables from the roasting pan to a sieve set over a medium saucepan.

2
Using a large spoon, skim the fat from the top of the meat juices.

3
Set the roasting pan over medium-high heat. When hot, add 1 cup chicken broth while stirring to loosen the bits from the pan bottom.

4
Pour the broth mixture over the vegetables in the sieve into the saucepan. Discard the veggies.

5
Add another 5 cups broth to the saucepan and bring to a simmer over medium-low heat.

6
In a small saucepan, warm ¼ cup butter over medium-low heat. Add ¼ cup flour and cook, stirring, for 2 minutes to make a roux.

7
Whisk 1 cup of the hot broth into the roux, then whisk the roux-broth mixture into the saucepan.

8
Bring the gravy mixture to a boil, then reduce the heat to medium-low. Simmer until thickened, about 5 minutes.

9
Transfer the gravy to a serving pitcher and serve warm alongside the turkey.

GINGER BEEF & SNOW PEA STIR-FRY

The key to a successful stir-fry is to prep all the ingredients before you start cooking. The dish will come together very quickly, so that means you have to be ready. Use a rounded wok spatula or a wooden spoon to stir and toss the ingredients while they quickly cook in the wok. Serve with soy sauce at the table.

1 MIX THE SAUCE

In a small bowl, mix the cornstarch and water, stirring until the cornstarch dissolves. Stir in the soy sauce, ginger, and garlic and set aside.

2 STIR-FRY THE SNOW PEAS

In a wok or frying pan, warm 1 tablespoon of the oil over high heat, swirling to coat the bottom and sides of the pan. When the oil is very hot but not quite smoking, add the snow peas and stir-fry, tossing every 10–15 seconds until just tender, about 2 minutes. Transfer to a large bowl and set aside.

3 STIR-FRY THE BEEF & BELL PEPPER

Add another 1 tablespoon oil to the pan, again swirling to coat the pan. When the oil is hot but not quite smoking, add half of the beef strips and stir-fry over high heat, stirring and spreading out the beef every 15–20 seconds, until lightly browned but still slightly pink inside, 2–3 minutes. Be sure to distribute the meat evenly in the pan so it cooks evenly. Transfer to a bowl. Add the remaining 1 tablespoon oil to the pan and stir-fry the remaining beef. Return the first batch of beef to the pan. Add the bell pepper and stir-fry over high heat until just beginning to wilt, 1–2 minutes.

4 ADD THE SAUCE

Quickly stir the cornstarch-soy mixture and add it to the pan. Cook, tossing the mixture occasionally, until the sauce thickens, 1–2 minutes. Return the snow peas to the pan and toss to coat evenly with the sauce. Serve with the steamed rice alongside.

2 teaspoons cornstarch

3 tablespoons water

3 tablespoons reduced-sodium soy sauce

1 teaspoon grated, peeled ginger

1 small clove garlic, minced

3 tablespoons peanut or vegetable oil

¼ lb snow peas or sugar snap peas

1 lb flank steak, cut in half lengthwise, then cut crosswise into thin slices

1 red bell pepper, seeded and cut into thin strips

2 cups steamed white or brown rice (page 123) for serving

PAN-FRIED STEAKS WITH THYME & GARLIC

If you're a meat lover, knowing how to cook a good steak is essential. The goal is to develop a nicely browned crusty exterior and pink, juicy interior—a feat that can be accomplished by allowing the steaks to cook, undisturbed, until well browned on the bottoms before turning them and timing it just right.

1 SEASON THE STEAKS

Pat the steaks dry with paper towels. Generously season both sides with salt and pepper. If the steaks have been refrigerated, bring them to room temperature for at least 15 minutes.

2 COOK THE STEAKS

Heat a wide, heavy-bottomed frying pan, preferably cast iron, over medium heat. Add the oil, swirl to coat the pan, then add the steaks. Cook, without moving, until well browned on the bottoms, about 4 minutes, decreasing the temperature slightly if the pan begins to smoke. Using tongs, carefully turn the steaks and continue to cook, without moving, until well browned on the second side, about 4 minutes longer. Use the tongs to turn the steaks again, reduce the heat to medium-low and add the butter, thyme, and garlic. Grasping the pan handle with an oven mitt, tilt the pan so the butter pools to one side. Continue to cook the steaks, using a large spoon to baste the steaks often with the butter, until medium-rare or a meat thermometer inserted into the center of each steak registers 135°F, or until done to your liking, about 1½ minutes longer. Transfer the steaks to a plate and let rest for 10 minutes.

3 SERVE THE STEAKS

Slice the steaks across the grain and serve, pouring any meat from the plate and remaining butter from the pan over the top.

2 boneless steaks, such as New York strip or filet mignon, each about ¾ lb and 1 inch thick, trimmed of excess fat

Kosher salt and freshly ground pepper

1 teaspoon olive oil

¼ cup unsalted butter

2 sprigs fresh thyme or 1 sprig fresh rosemary

2 cloves garlic, crushed

» LET THE MEAT REST for 10 minutes after cooking so the juices can redistribute, resulting in meat that is tender and juicy. Then cut the meat across the grain into slices.

GRILLED PORK CHOPS WITH NECTARINE SALSA

Soaking tougher cuts of meat in a salty brine solution can bring extra tenderness and flavor to the meat, but it is not essential. For meaty chops with bones, fatty cuts, or slow-cooking meats, set up a grill for indirect-heat cooking to prevent burning and promote even cooking.

1 BRINE THE PORK CHOPS (OPTIONAL)

Place the pork chops in a large lock-top plastic bag and pour in the brine. Seal the bag closed, squish the brine around the chops, and refrigerate overnight. The next day, remove the bag from the refrigerator at least 30 minutes before grilling. Discard the brine, rinse the chops briefly in cold water, and pat dry with paper towels.

2 PREPARE THE GRILL

Prepare a charcoal or gas grill for indirect-heat grilling over medium heat (350°–375°F). If using charcoal, bank the lit coals on either side of the grill bed, leaving a strip in the center without heat. If using gas, preheat the burners, then turn off 1 or more of the burners to create a cooler zone. Oil the grill rack.

3 GRILL THE CHOPS

Place the pork chops on the grill over the direct-heat area and sear, turning once, until nicely grill-marked on both sides, 2–3 minutes on each side. Move the chops to the indirect-heat area, cover the grill, and cook until the chops are somewhat firm to the touch and an instant-read thermometer inserted into the center of a chop away from the bone registers 145°F for medium, about 15 minutes.

4 SERVE THE CHOPS

Transfer the chops to a platter and let rest for 10 minutes, then serve with the nectarine salsa.

6 bone-in pork chops, at least 1 inch thick

About 6 cups Basic Pork Brine (page 122), optional

Canola oil for the grill

1½ cups Nectarine Salsa (page 125)

GRILLED SHRIMP TACOS WITH PINEAPPLE-JICAMA SALSA

Pineapple might seem like an odd ingredient for fresh salsa, but when it is infused with chile, its spicy-sweet character makes it the perfect partner for grilled shrimp. If you can't find fresh pineapple, mango or melon could stand in. This recipe can easily be doubled to serve a crowd.

1 MAKE THE SALSA

In a nonaluminum bowl, gently toss together the pineapple, jicama, cilantro, onion, jalapeño (if using), olive oil, and lime juice. Season to taste with salt and pepper. Set aside at room temperature until ready to serve or refrigerate in an airtight container for up to 1 day.

2 GRILL THE SHRIMP

Heat a nonstick grill pan over medium-high heat or prepare a charcoal or gas grill for direct-heat cooking over medium-high heat. Oil the grill pan or grill rack. Thread the shrimp onto long metal skewers. In a small bowl, mix together the grapeseed oil, chile powder, and garlic. Brush the shrimp with some of the oil mixture. Using tongs, place the shrimp skewers on the grill pan or grill rack and grill, turning once, until bright pink and opaque throughout, about 4 minutes total. Transfer to a plate.

3 GRILL THE TORTILLAS

Lightly brush the tortillas with the remaining oil mixture and place on the grill pan or grill rack. Grill, turning once with tongs, until puffy on both sides, about 2 minutes total.

4 ASSEMBLE THE TACOS

Place 2 tortillas on each of 4 warmed plates. Remove the shrimp from the skewers and arrange them in the center of each tortilla, dividing them evenly, and top each portion with a large spoonful of the salsa. Serve, passing the remaining salsa at the table.

FOR THE SALSA

½ pineapple, peeled, cored, and diced (about 2½ cups)

1 cup peeled and diced jicama

½ cup loosely packed fresh cilantro leaves, chopped

⅓ cup finely chopped red onion

1 small jalapeño chile, seeded and minced (optional)

2 tablespoons olive oil

1 tablespoon fresh lime juice

Kosher salt and freshly ground pepper

FOR THE SHRIMP TACOS

2 tablespoons grapeseed or canola oil, plus oil for the grill

1 lb medium shrimp, peeled and deveined

½ teaspoon chipotle chile powder

1 small clove garlic, minced

8 taco-size corn tortillas

PIZZA WITH CARAMELIZED ONION, BELL PEPPERS & BACON

To shape the dough, pick up the dough disk gently near the edge, allowing it to hang and stretch. Move your hands along the edge to expand the width of the disk.

1 PREHEAT THE OVEN
Set a pizza stone on a rack in the lower third of the oven. Preheat the oven to 450°F.

2 CARAMELIZE THE ONIONS
Warm the olive oil in a frying pan over medium heat. Add the onion, stir to coat well, and season to taste with salt and pepper. Cook, stirring often, until the onion is a rich caramel color, about 30 minutes. Add the garlic and cook, stirring, for about 1 minute. Remove from the heat and set aside.

3 SHAPE THE DOUGH
Sprinkle cornmeal over a pizza peel or the flat side of a rimless baking sheet. Place the dough round on the peel or sheet. Press and stretch the dough into a 10- to 12-inch disk. If the dough springs back as you shape it, let it rest for 5–10 minutes, then continue.

4 ADD THE TOPPINGS
Spread the pizza sauce evenly over the dough, then scatter the onions, cheese, peppers, bacon, corn, and olives over the top.

5 BAKE THE PIZZA
Gently shake the peel to loosen the pizza. Place the rounded end of the peel over the far side of the pizza stone. Tip the peel to allow the pizza to fall onto the stone while slipping the peel from underneath the pizza. Bake until the bottom of the crust is crisp and the top is blistered, about 10 minutes. Let cool for 5 minutes. Sprinkle with basil, then slice and serve.

1 round Basic Pizza Dough (page 76) or store-bought refrigerated pizza dough, at room temperature

1 tablespoon olive oil

1 yellow onion, cut in half through the stem end and thinly sliced crosswise

Salt and freshly ground pepper

1 large clove garlic, minced

Cornmeal for dusting

⅓ cup store-bought pizza sauce

¼ lb shredded mozzarella cheese

¼ cup sweet mini bell peppers, cored, seeded, and thinly sliced

2 tablespoons chopped cooked bacon

2 tablespoons frozen corn, thawed

1 tablespoon chopped pitted kalamata olives

Small fresh basil leaves for garnish

BASIC PIZZA DOUGH

makes
3
rounds

To store any leftover dough, seal the oven-ready dough in a lock-top plastic bag and refrigerate for up to 2 days or freeze for up to 2 months. Bring to room temperature (about 30 minutes if refrigerated or 3 hours if frozen) before using.

1 MIX THE DOUGH

In a bowl, sprinkle the yeast on top of the water and let stand until dissolved, about 5 minutes. Using a wooden spoon, stir in the salt, oil, and 3 cups of the flour until combined.

2 KNEAD THE DOUGH

Scatter another ½ cup flour on a work surface and dump the dough onto the flour. Using well-floured hands, knead the dough: fold the dough towards you in half, then push it away from you with the heel of your hand. Turn the dough a quarter turn, then fold and push again until the dough is smooth and springy, 10–15 minutes, adding up to ½ cup more flour as needed to prevent sticking.

3 LET IT RISE

Oil a large bowl, place the dough in the bowl, and turn to oil the top. Cover the bowl with plastic wrap and let the dough rise at room temperature until doubled in bulk, about 45 minutes, or in the refrigerator for up to 12 hours. Once risen, dump out the dough onto a lightly floured work surface and press out the air. Cover with a kitchen towel and let rest for 10 minutes. Cut into 3 equal pieces. Gently shape each piece into a round. Top and bake (see page 75).

1½ cups lukewarm water (about 110°F)

1 package (about 2¼ teaspoons) active dry yeast

½ teaspoon salt

1 tablespoon olive oil, plus more for oiling bowl

About 4 cups all-purpose flour

1 Stir the flour into the yeast mixture until combined.

2 To knead the dough, fold then push with the heel of your hand. Turn the dough, then fold and push again.

3 The dough has been kneaded enough when it springs back into place after being depressed with a fingertip.

CHEESY BEEF TACO-STUFFED AVOCADO

Large, ripe Hass avocados are the best choice for this easy dish. Once hollowed, filled, and baked, one generous avocado half makes the perfect size for a satisfying lunch or light dinner. If large avocados are unavailable, fill and serve two smaller avocado halves per person.

1 COOK THE BEEF

Preheat the oven to 450°F. Heat a large frying pan over medium heat. Add the ground beef and cook, using a wooden spoon to break up the meat into small pieces, until no longer pink, about 3 minutes. (Ask an adult to help you pour off any fat from the pan if it looks greasy.) Add the seasoning mix and water to the pan. Bring to a boil over high heat. Reduce the heat to low and simmer, stirring often, until the liquid is absorbed, about 12 minutes.

2 STUFF THE AVOCADOS

Cut each avocado in half lengthwise and remove the pits. Using a spoon, scoop out a hollow in each avocado half about 2 inches wide and 1 inch deep. Place the avocados, cut side up, on a rimmed baking sheet. (If necessary, cut a thin slice from the rounded side of each avocado half to prevent wobbling.) Spoon an equal amount of the beans, taco meat, and tomatoes into each avocado half, then top each with a slice of cheese.

3 MELT THE CHEESE

Bake the avocados until the cheese melts and the filling is heated through, about 3 minutes. Serve hot.

¾ lb ground beef

3 tablespoons taco seasoning mix

½ cup water

2 large, ripe avocados

¼ cup canned refried beans, warmed

2 plum tomatoes, diced

4 slices (about 2 oz) Cheddar cheese

BURRITO BOWL

You can customize this bowl with your favorite burrito ingredients. If the chicken breasts are thick, use a flat meat mallet to pound them to an even 1-inch thickness. Or, for a faster, easier meal, use shredded rotisserie chicken instead.

1 MARINATE THE CHICKEN

In a large lock-top plastic bag, combine the marinade and chicken. Seal the bag and let the chicken marinate in the refrigerator for at least 2 hours or up to overnight.

2 GRILL THE CHICKEN

Prepare a charcoal or gas grill for direct-heat cooking over medium heat (about 400°F) or heat a stovetop grill pan over medium heat. Brush the grill grates or grill pan with oil. Grill the chicken, turning once, until grill marks appear on both sides, the meat is opaque throughout when cut with a knife, and a meat thermometer inserted into the thickest part of the breast registers 165°F, about 12 minutes total. Transfer to a cutting board and let rest while you prepare the bowls.

3 SEASON THE RICE

To the rice, add the lime zest, 2 tablespoons of the lime juice, and the cilantro. Fluff with a fork. Season to taste with salt. Keep warm.

4 WARM THE CORN & BEANS

In a frying pan, warm the olive oil over medium heat. Add the beans and remaining 1 tablespoon lime juice to the pan and cook, stirring, until heated through, about 2 minutes. Season to taste with salt.

5 ASSEMBLE THE BOWLS

Cut the chicken into bite-size pieces. Divide the rice among 4 bowls. Top with equal amounts of the chicken, beans, corn, guacamole, salsa, and cheese. Sprinkle with cilantro and serve with lime wedges on the side.

FOR THE CHICKEN
½ cup Adobo Marinade (page 122)
1¼ lb boneless, skinless chicken breasts (2 or 3 breasts)
Canola oil for the grill

3 cups steamed white or brown rice (page 123), warm
½ teaspoon grated lime zest
3 tablespoons fresh lime juice
2 tablespoons finely chopped fresh cilantro
Salt
1 tablespoon olive oil
1 can (15 oz) black or pinto beans, rinsed and drained
⅔ cup corn kernels
½ cup guacamole
½ cup salsa or pico de gallo
¾ cup shredded Monterey jack cheese
Chopped fresh cilantro
Lime wedges

RAMEN BOWL WITH EDAMAME

Ramen bowls are revered as much for their artful arrangement of ingredients as they are for their multilayered flavor. Select the best-quality ingredients you can find, then take your time when arranging them in each bowl.

1 COOK THE NOODLES

In a large pot, combine the chicken broth, water, soy sauce, ketchup, and chili oil (if using). Bring to a boil over medium-high heat, then add the noodles and mushrooms. Reduce the heat to medium-low and simmer until the noodles are tender (check the package for the cooking time).

2 ASSEMBLE THE BOWLS

Divide the noodles and broth among 6 bowls. Immediately add the pork slices, immersing them into the liquid in each bowl so that they cook in the hot broth. Divide the eggs, tomatoes, radishes, and edamame evenly among the bowls, sprinkle each serving with fresh herbs, and serve hot.

4 cups reduced-sodium chicken broth

2 cups water

¼ cup reduced-sodium soy sauce

3 tablespoons ketchup

⅛ teaspoon chili oil (optional)

9 oz ramen noodles

8 oz shiitake, cremini, or white mushrooms, caps thinly sliced

6 oz thinly sliced pork tenderloin

6 Soft-Boiled Eggs (page 22)

12 cherry tomatoes, halved

3 radishes, thinly sliced

½ cup thawed frozen edamame

Chopped fresh herbs, such as mint, basil, and cilantro, for garnish

CLASSIC PASTA CARBONARA

In this classic pasta from Rome, a luxurious egg sauce cooks while being tossed with hot pasta, evenly coating each noodle. The pasta should be hot enough to cook the eggs in the sauce, but not so hot that the eggs become scrambled.

1 COOK THE PASTA

Bring a large pot of salted water to a boil. Add the pasta, stir, and cook according to the package directions, stirring occasionally, until al dente.

2 MAKE THE SAUCE

While the pasta is cooking, in a sauté pan, warm the olive oil over medium heat. Add the bacon and cook, stirring occasionally, until browned and slightly crisp, 3–5 minutes. Pour off all but 1½ tablespoons of the fat. Set aside the pan with the bacon and reserved fat. In a small bowl, beat the eggs with a fork to loosen them, add the nutmeg (if using), and season to taste with salt.

3 MIX THE PASTA & SAUCE

Drain the pasta, reserving ¼ cup of the pasta cooking water. Warm the pan with the bacon over medium heat and add the pasta. Using tongs, thoroughly toss the pasta with the bacon and fat and season to taste with salt. Remove the pan from the heat, add the egg mixture, and quickly toss with the hot pasta to thicken the sauce without scrambling the eggs. If the sauce seems dry, add 1 or 2 tablespoons of the reserved pasta cooking water and toss again.

4 SERVE THE PASTA

Divide the pasta among warmed shallow bowls, grate the cheese and coarsely grind pepper over each bowl, and serve.

1 lb linguine, spaghettini, fedelini, or other long noodles

2 tablespoons olive oil

6 thick bacon slices, chopped

4 large eggs

½ teaspoon freshly grated nutmeg (optional)

Salt and freshly ground pepper

Freshly grated pecorino romano or Parmesan cheese for serving

» TAMARIND PASTE is the fruit extracted from the pods of a tropical tree. It adds a distinctive sweet-sour flavor to Thai dishes. If unavailable, ketchup is the best substitute.

PAD THAI

This stir-fried rice noodle dish is a favorite street food in Thailand and a menu staple in any Thai restaurant. The combo of chewy noodles, a tangy-sweet sauce, and crunchy bean sprouts is irresistible wherever you eat it!

1 SOAK THE NOODLES

Fill a large saucepan three-quarters full with water and bring to a boil over high heat. Remove the pan from the heat, add the noodles, and stir well. Let the noodles soften in the hot water until tender but not mushy, 5–10 minutes. Drain the noodles and set aside.

2 FLAVOR THE NOODLES

In a small bowl, combine the fish sauce, tamarind, and sugar and stir until the sugar dissolves; set aside. Heat the oil in a large frying pan over medium heat for about 1 minute. Add the garlic and cook, stirring constantly, until golden, about 30 seconds. Add the eggs and cook without stirring until barely set, about 30 seconds. Add the drained noodles and cook, stirring, for 2 minutes. Add ¾ cup of the bean sprouts, half of the green onions, and the shrimp and cook, stirring constantly, until just heated through, 1–2 minutes. Pour in the fish sauce mixture and stir to combine.

3 SERVE THE PAD THAI

Transfer the pad thai to a platter. Sprinkle with the remaining bean sprouts and green onions, the peanuts, and the cilantro. Serve with lime wedges on the side.

½ lb dried flat rice noodles

3 tablespoons fish sauce

1½ tablespoons tamarind paste or ketchup

1 tablespoon sugar

2 tablespoons vegetable oil

3 cloves garlic, minced

2 large eggs, lightly beaten

1 cup bean sprouts

3 green onions, thinly sliced

1 cup peeled and cooked small shrimp

2 tablespoons chopped unsalted roasted peanuts

3 tablespoons chopped fresh cilantro

Lime wedges for serving

TANDOORI CHICKEN THIGHS WITH COCONUT-GREEN ONION RICE

This Indian dish is traditionally cooked in a *tandoor,* the round charcoal-fueled clay oven from which it gets its name. A stove-top grill pan yields similar results.

1 MARINATE THE CHICKEN

In a large bowl, stir together the yogurt, tomato paste, lemon juice, garam masala, turmeric, salt, and cayenne. Add the chicken to the bowl and toss to coat well. Cover and refrigerate for 30 minutes.

2 GRILL THE CHICKEN

Coat a nonstick grill pan with cooking spray, place over medium-high heat, and let heat for 2 minutes. Add half of the chicken thighs to the pan in a single layer. Cook, turning once, until grill marks appear on both sides, the meat is opaque throughout when carefully cut into with a knife, and a meat thermometer inserted into the thickest part of the thigh registers 165°F, 4–8 minutes total. (Alternatively, you can roast the chicken thighs on a rack in a roasting pan in a preheated 375°F oven for about 30 minutes.)

3 SERVE THE CHICKEN & RICE

Transfer the chicken to a serving dish and cover to keep warm. Repeat with the remaining chicken thighs, adding them to the dish when they are done. Serve the chicken with the rice alongside. Pass the sauce for adding at the table.

¾ cup plain whole-milk yogurt

1 tablespoon tomato paste

1 tablespoon fresh lemon juice

2 teaspoons garam masala

1 teaspoon ground turmeric

1 teaspoon salt

¼ teaspoon cayenne pepper

2 lb boneless, skinless chicken thighs

Cooking spray

3 cups Coconut–Green Onion Rice (page 123)

1 cup Yogurt Sauce (page 124)

COCONUT GREEN CURRY WITH CHICKEN & SWEET POTATOES

Of the three Thai-style curry pastes—red, yellow, and green—green is the mildest. Feel free to sub in the yellow or red if you prefer a spicier dish.

1 **BOIL THE POTATOES**

Bring a large pot of salted water to a boil over high heat. Add the sweet potatoes and cook until fork-tender, about 6 minutes. Drain well, transfer to a large bowl, and set aside.

2 **COOK THE CHICKEN**

Warm 1 tablespoon of the oil in a large, heavy-bottomed saucepan over medium-high heat. Season the chicken all over with salt and pepper. Add it to the hot oil and cook, stirring a few times, until browned on all sides, about 4 minutes total. Using a slotted spoon, transfer to a plate and set aside. Do not wipe out the pan.

3 **COOK THE BELL PEPPER**

Add the remaining 1 tablespoon oil to the same pan. Add the onion and bell pepper, season with salt and pepper, and cook, stirring, until the vegetables are soft, about 4 minutes. Stir in the garlic and ginger and cook, stirring, for 2 minutes. Transfer the onion–bell pepper mixture to the bowl with the sweet potatoes. Do not wipe out the pan.

4 **MAKE THE CURRY**

Open the coconut milk can, but do not shake it. Spoon out the thick cream from the top of the can and add it to the saucepan along with the green curry paste; stir to combine. Whisk in the rest of the coconut milk, the broth, and the fish sauce and bring to a simmer over medium-high heat. Return the chicken to the pan and cook until opaque throughout, about 8 minutes. Add the sweet potatoes and other vegetables and cook just until warmed through, about 5 minutes longer. Stir in the basil and serve with steamed rice.

1 lb sweet potatoes, peeled and cut into ½-inch cubes

2 tablespoons canola oil

1 lb boneless, skinless chicken thighs, cut into ½-inch pieces

Salt and freshly ground pepper

1 yellow onion, cut into 8 wedges

1 red bell pepper, seeded and cut into ½-inch-wide strips

3 cloves garlic, minced

2-inch knob fresh ginger, peeled and minced

1 can (14 oz) coconut milk

2 tablespoons green curry paste

1 cup reduced-sodium chicken broth

2 tablespoons fish sauce

4 fresh basil leaves, chopped

Steamed white or brown rice (page 123)

5-LAYER LASAGNA BOLOGNESE

Either fresh pasta sheets or oven-ready lasagna noodles cook perfectly in this classic lasagna. Rinse oven-ready noodles in hot water before using them.

1 MAKE THE BOLOGNESE

Warm the oil in a large, heavy frying pan over medium-low heat. Add the onion and cook, stirring, until translucent, about 5 minutes. Add the celery and carrot and cook, stirring, until tender, about 10 minutes. Add the ground beef and cook, breaking up the beef with a wooden spoon, until no longer pink, 5-10 minutes. Stir in the milk and simmer until evaporated, about 8 minutes. Add the tomatoes and tomato sauce and season to taste with salt and red pepper flakes. Bring to a simmer over medium heat. Reduce the heat to low and simmer, stirring often, until the sauce is thick, about 2 hours.

2 MAKE THE BÉCHAMEL

Melt the butter in a saucepan over medium heat. Add the shallots and cook, stirring, until soft, about 5 minutes. Add the flour and cook, stirring frequently, for 3 minutes; do not brown. Using a whisk, gradually whisk in the milk and half-and-half. Reduce the heat to medium-low and simmer, stirring often, until the sauce thickens, about 8 minutes. Remove from the heat and season to taste with salt and white pepper. Remove from the heat and set aside.

3 ASSEMBLE AND BAKE THE LASAGNA

Meanwhile, preheat the oven to 350°F. Butter a 9 x 13-inch baking dish. To assemble, spread ½ cup of béchamel in the bottom of the baking dish. Top with a single layer of pasta, one-quarter of the Bolognese, another ½ cup of the béchamel, and ¼ cup of the Parmesan. Repeat three more times with layers of pasta, Bolognese, béchamel, and Parmesan. Finish with a final layer of pasta to make 5 layers total, then the remaining béchamel and Parmesan. Bake until lightly browned and the sauce is bubbling, about 30 minutes. Let stand for 10 minutes, then cut into squares.

FOR THE BOLOGNESE

3 tablespoons olive oil

1 yellow onion, finely chopped

1 celery stalk, finely chopped

1 small carrot, finely chopped

1 lb *each* lean ground beef and ground pork or veal

¾ cup milk

1 can (28 oz) diced tomatoes with juices

¾ cup tomato sauce

Salt

Red pepper flakes

FOR THE BÉCHAMEL

¼ cup unsalted butter

2 shallots, peeled and minced

¼ cup all-purpose flour

2 cups whole milk

1 cup half-and-half

Salt and ground white pepper

FOR THE LASAGNA

Butter for greasing

12 oz oven-ready lasagna noodles (see note above) or 1 lb fresh pasta sheets

1¼ cups grated Parmesan cheese

» GREAT FOR LEFTOVERS
and for making ahead, lasagna
is at its very best when cooked,
cooled, and refrigerated, then
rewarmed before serving.

FOIL-PACKET COD WITH TOMATOES, OLIVES & SPINACH

Cooking fish inside a foil packet steams the fish while infusing it with all the flavors inside. Even better, this method is completely hands-off. Wrap all the ingredients in a piece of foil, seal, and bake: In 15 minutes, your meal is ready.

1 PREHEAT THE OVEN
Preheat the oven to 375°F. Place a 12-inch piece of aluminum foil on a rimmed baking sheet.

2 MAKE THE FOIL PACKET
Scatter the spinach over half of the foil. Drizzle 1½ teaspoons of the oil over the spinach and season to taste with salt and pepper. Place the cod fillet on the spinach and top with the tomatoes, olives, and rosemary. Drizzle with the remaining 1½ teaspoons oil, season generously with salt and pepper, and squeeze the lemon wedge over the top. Fold the uncovered half of the foil over the fish and crimp the edges to seal the fish inside.

3 BAKE THE FISH
Bake until the fish is opaque throughout, about 15 minutes. Open the foil packet carefully (hot steam will come out as soon as you unseal it) and transfer the fish and vegetables to a plate. Drizzle with the salsa verde (if using) and serve.

1 cup firmly packed baby spinach

1 tablespoon olive oil

Salt and freshly ground pepper

1 cod fillet (about 6 oz)

5 cherry tomatoes, halved

2 tablespoons cured black olives, pitted and halved

½ tsp dried rosemary

1 lemon wedge

2 tablespoons Salsa Verde (page 124), optional

CHEDDAR, PEAR & PROSCIUTTO PANINI

Thin slices of firm, fruity Bosc pear may seem an uncommon addition to a grilled cheese sandwich, but they create the perfect balance of flavors when paired with salty prosciutto and a good sharp Cheddar.

1 CUT THE PEARS

Stand the pears upright on a cutting surface and cut them lengthwise into thin slices, stopping to rotate the pear when you hit the seedy core.

2 ASSEMBLE THE SANDWICHES

Lay 2 bread slices on a work surface and top each with 1 slice of the cheese. Divide the prosciutto and pear evenly over the cheese, then top each stack with another slice of cheese. Spread the remaining 2 bread slices with the pesto (if using) and place them, pesto side down, over the cheese on each sandwich. Spread the top and bottom of each sandwich with ½ tablespoon of the butter.

3 GRILL THE SANDWICHES

Return the frying pan to medium heat or heat a panini press. Add the sandwiches. Place a flat lid or a heatproof plate on the sandwiches in the frying pan to weight them down or close the panini press. Cook, turning once (and replacing the weight if a frying pan is being used), until golden brown on both sides, about 4 minutes total. Cut each sandwich into halves and serve.

2 Bosc pears or other firm pears

2 everything bagels or brioche buns, halved

4 thin slices (about ¼ lb) sharp white Cheddar cheese, thinly sliced

4 thin slices (about ¼ lb) prosciutto or 4 slices cooked bacon, halved crosswise

2 tablespoons Fresh Basil Pesto (page 124) or store-bought pesto (optional)

2 tablespoons unsalted butter, at room temperature

POTATO GNOCCHI WITH BASIL PESTO

The little Italian potato dumplings known as gnocchi are easier to make than fresh pasta and just as tasty. Serve them with basil pesto (as here) or tomato sauce, or simply toss them with melted butter and plenty of grated Parmesan.

1 BAKE & MASH THE POTATOES

Preheat the oven to 375°F. Using a fork, poke holes in 4 or 5 places all over each potato. Place the potatoes directly on the oven rack and bake until tender, about 1 hour. Remove from the oven and set aside until cool enough to handle, then cut the potatoes in half lengthwise and use a spoon to scoop the flesh into a bowl. Using a potato ricer or potato masher, mash the potatoes. Let cool.

2 MIX THE DOUGH

In a cup, lightly beat the egg yolks and salt. When the potatoes are cool, stir in the egg mixture. Add the flour, ½ cup at a time, using a large spoon to mix the dough until smooth but still sticky before adding more.

3 SHAPE THE DOUGH

Divide the dough into pieces the size of tennis balls. Shape as directed in steps 4–6 (at right), continuing until all are shaped.

4 COOK THE GNOCCHI

Bring a large pot of salted water to a boil over high heat. Add half of the gnocchi and cook until they float to the surface, about 3 minutes. Using a slotted spoon, transfer the cooked gnocchi to a warmed serving bowl. Cook the remaining gnocchi in the same way, adding them to the bowl when they are cooked.

5 SERVE THE GNOCCHI

Drain any water collected in the bowl. Spoon the pesto over the gnocchi and toss to coat. Divide the gnocchi among 6 bowls. Serve with Parmesan for adding at the table.

2 lb russet potatoes

2 large egg yolks

2 teaspoons salt

About 2 cups all-purpose flour

1 cup Fresh Basil Pesto (page 124)

Freshly grated Parmesan cheese for serving

HOW TO MAKE POTATO GNOCCHI

1

Using a fork, poke holes in 4 or 5 places all over each potato.

2

Using a potato ricer or potato masher, mash the baked potatoes in the bowl.

3

Add the flour, ½ cup at a time, using a large spoon to mix the dough.

4

Work with one ball of dough at a time; keep the remaining dough covered with an overturned bowl. On a floured surface, roll the ball of dough into a rope about ½ inch thick.

5

Using a kitchen knife, cut each rope into ¾-inch pieces.

6

With the tip of an index finger, press each dough piece gently against the tines of a fork while swiping down, allowing the gnocchi to roll off and fall onto the work surface.

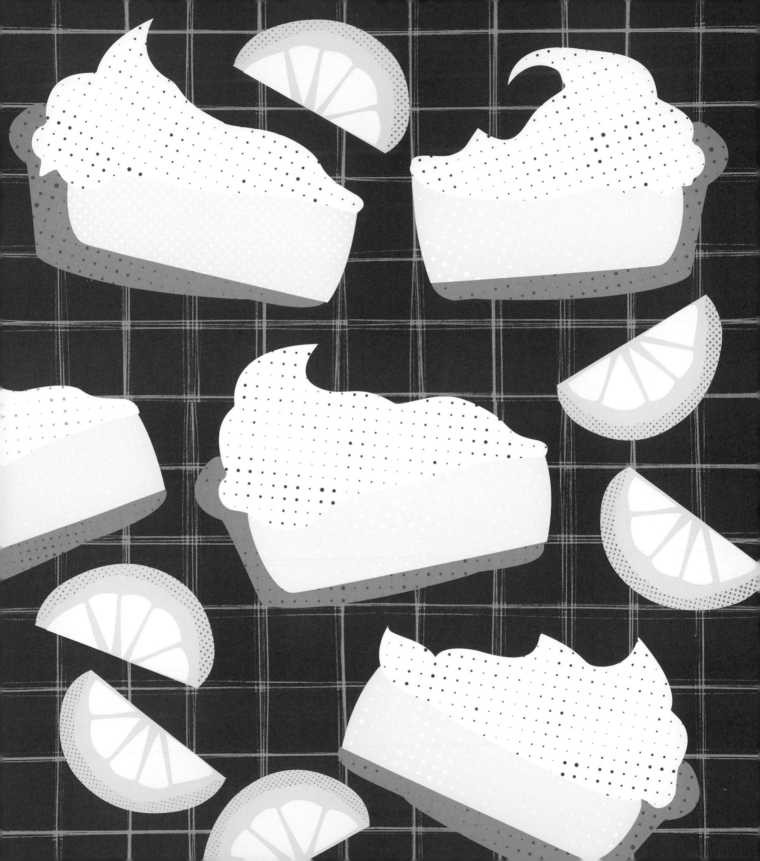

DESSERTS

CHOCOLATE-DIPPED PEANUT BUTTER HI-HAT CUPCAKES

A double dose of chocolate—in the form of cocoa powder and chopped bittersweet chocolate—makes these cupcakes extra rich. Topped with light and fluffy peanut butter–kissed frosting and then dipped in more melted chocolate, these treats look as decadent as they taste.

1 PREPARE THE PAN

Preheat the oven to 350°F. Line a standard 12-cup muffin pan with paper or foil liners.

2 MIX THE DRY INGREDIENTS

In a bowl, whisk together the flour, cocoa powder, baking powder, and salt. Set aside.

3 MELT THE CHOCOLATE

In a microwave-safe bowl, combine the butter and chopped chocolate. Microwave on high power, stirring every 20 seconds, just until the mixture is melted and smooth. Let the mixture cool until barely warm, 10–15 minutes.

4 MAKE THE BATTER

Whisk the granulated sugar into the chocolate mixture until combined. Add the eggs one at a time, whisking well after each addition. Add the vanilla and mix until blended. Add the flour mixture and mix just until combined and no traces of flour remain; do not overmix.

5 BAKE THE CUPCAKES

Divide the batter evenly among the prepared muffin cups. Bake until a toothpick inserted into the center of a cupcake comes out

Continued on page 96 »

FOR THE CUPCAKES

⅔ cup all-purpose flour

3 tablespoons unsweetened cocoa powder, sifted

1 teaspoon baking powder

¼ teaspoon salt

11 tablespoons unsalted butter, cut into pieces

3 oz bittersweet chocolate, chopped

¾ cup granulated sugar

3 large eggs

1 teaspoon pure vanilla extract

» *Continued from page 94*

with only a few crumbs attached, 22–24 minutes. Set the pan on a wire rack and let cool for 10 minutes. Transfer the cupcakes directly to the rack and let cool completely.

6 MAKE THE FROSTING

In the bowl of a stand mixer, preferably using the paddle attachment, beat the butter on medium-high speed until fluffy, about 3 minutes. Add the peanut butter, powdered sugar, and vanilla and beat until smooth and well combined, scraping down the sides of the bowl as needed. Add the marshmallow crème and beat until smooth.

7 FILL THE PIPING BAG

Place a pastry bag fitted with a ½-inch round tip (or a plastic bag with a ½-inch hole snipped in a corner) tip-end down in a glass. Fold back the open end of the bag over the sides of the glass to hold it open. Spoon the frosting into the bag and secure closed.

8 FROST THE CUPCAKES

Pipe ¼–⅓ cup frosting onto each cupcake in a swirl (it should look like soft-serve ice cream). Place the frosted cupcakes back in the muffin pan and refrigerate the cupcakes until the frosting is firm, about 1 hour.

9 DIP THE CUPCAKES

In a small saucepan, bring about 1 inch of water to a simmer over medium-low heat. In a heatproof bowl that is slightly larger than the saucepan, combine the chocolate chips and oil. Place the bowl on the saucepan, making sure that the bowl does not touch the simmering water below. Heat the chocolate, stirring often, until melted and smooth, 3–4 minutes. One at a time, dip the cupcakes, frosted end down, into the melted chocolate, then place on a serving platter. Let the frosting set for about 15 minutes, then serve.

FOR THE FROSTING

¾ cup unsalted butter,
at room temperature

½ cup creamy peanut butter

1½ cups powdered sugar, sifted

1 teaspoon pure vanilla extract

1 jar (7 oz) marshmallow crème

FOR THE CHOCOLATE DIP

1⅓ cups (about 8 oz)
semisweet chocolate chips

1½ tablespoons canola oil

CLASSIC CRÈME BRÛLÉE

The key to this traditional dessert is to stir the custard continuously over low heat so that the eggs don't scramble during cooking. A small kitchen torch is the easiest way to caramelize the sugar topping, although a broiler will work in a pinch. Always have an adult nearby when working with a flame of any kind.

1 BEAT THE CREAM & EGGS

In a saucepan over medium heat, warm the cream until small bubbles appear around the edges of the pan. Meanwhile, in a heatproof bowl, using an electric mixer on high speed or a whisk, beat together the egg yolks and granulated sugar until pale yellow and thick enough to fall from the beaters or whisk in a lazy ribbon, about 5 minutes with a mixer or 8 minutes with a whisk.

2 COOK THE CUSTARD

Pour about 1 inch of water into a small saucepan and bring to a simmer over medium-low heat. While whisking constantly, gradually pour the hot cream into the egg yolk mixture. Place the bowl on the saucepan, making sure that the bowl does not touch the simmering water below, and cook, stirring constantly with a wooden spoon, until the custard thickens and lightly coats the back of a spoon, 5–10 minutes. Do not allow to boil. Remove the bowl from the pan and stir in the vanilla. Strain the custard through a fine-mesh sieve into a large glass measuring cup with a spout.

3 CHILL THE CUSTARD

Divide the custard among 6 ovenproof ½-cup ramekins. Let cool, cover, and refrigerate for at least 2 hours or up to overnight.

4 CARAMELIZE THE SUGAR

Preheat the broiler or ready a kitchen torch. Sift a thin coating of brown sugar over the top of each custard, covering the surface evenly. Slip the custards under the broiler or move the torch in a figure-eight motion over each custard until the sugar is evenly browned and melted, then serve.

3 cups heavy cream

6 large egg yolks

2 tablespoons granulated sugar

½ teaspoon pure vanilla extract

Golden brown sugar for sifting

STICKY LEMON BUNDT CAKE

This dense, lemony cake gets a sweet, sticky coating from a lemon-infused sugar syrup that is liberally brushed over the top. Serve with whipped cream.

1 PREPARE THE PAN
Preheat the oven to 350°F. Lightly butter a 10-cup Bundt pan. Dust with flour and tap out the excess.

2 MIX THE BATTER
In a large bowl, sift together the flour, baking powder, and salt. Set aside. In an electric stand mixer fitted with the paddle attachment, cream together the butter and cream cheese on medium-high speed until smooth, about 3 minutes. Reduce the speed to medium, add the sugar, and beat until fluffy, about 2 minutes longer. Add the eggs one at a time, beating well after each addition. Remove the bowl and, using a spatula, fold in the flour mixture until incorporated. Stir in the vanilla, lemon zest, and lemon juice.

3 BAKE THE CAKE
Pour the batter into the prepared pan and smooth the top with the spatula. Bake until a toothpick inserted into the center comes out clean, about 1 hour.

4 MAKE THE SYRUP
Meanwhile, in a nonaluminum saucepan, combine the lemon zest, juice, and sugar over medium heat, stirring until the sugar is dissolved. Bring to a boil, then reduce the heat to low. Simmer until reduced by one-third, 10–15 minutes. Remove from the heat and set aside.

5 BRUSH WITH SYRUP
Transfer the cake to a wire rack and let cool in the pan for 30 minutes. Invert the cake onto a plate. While the cake is still warm, poke holes in the surface with a toothpick, then brush all over with all of the lemon syrup. Let cool for 30 minutes longer, then serve.

1½ cups unsalted butter, at room temperature, plus butter for greasing

3 cups all-purpose flour, plus flour for dusting

2 teaspoons baking powder

1 teaspoon salt

8 oz cream cheese, at room temperature

2 cups sugar

6 large eggs

2 teaspoons pure vanilla extract

1 tablespoon finely grated lemon zest

¼ cup fresh lemon juice

FOR THE LEMON SYRUP
1 tablespoon finely grated lemon zest

½ cup fresh lemon juice

½ cup sugar

CHERRY CRISP

A crisp is a baked fruit dessert with a crunchy topping of oats, flour, and sugar. This crisp is delicious on its own, but vanilla ice cream makes it irresistible!

1 PREPARE THE BAKING DISH
Preheat the oven to 375°F. Butter a 2-quart glass baking dish.

2 MAKE THE TOPPING
In a bowl, stir together the butter, brown sugar, cinnamon, and salt until combined. Stir in the oats and flour. Cover with plastic wrap and refrigerate while you make the filling.

3 MAKE THE FILLING
Set a colander over the sink and put the cherries in the colander to drain off any liquid. Transfer the drained cherries to a large bowl and stir in the vanilla. Sprinkle in the granulated sugar, cornstarch, and salt and stir to combine.

4 BAKE THE CRISP
Transfer the cherry mixture to the prepared baking dish and spread it out evenly. Remove the topping from the refrigerator and sprinkle it evenly over the fruit. Bake until the filling is bubbling and the topping is brown, 30–35 minutes. Let cool on a wire rack for about 20 minutes.

5 SERVE THE CRISP
Scoop portions of the warm crisp onto dessert plates. Top each serving with ice cream and serve.

FOR THE TOPPING

4 tablespoons unsalted butter, at room temperature, plus butter for greasing

¼ cup firmly packed golden brown sugar

½ teaspoon ground cinnamon

Pinch of salt

½ cup old-fashioned oats

½ cup all-purpose flour

FOR THE FILLING

2 lbs frozen pitted cherries, thawed

1 teaspoon pure vanilla extract

½ cup granulated sugar

1 tablespoon cornstarch

Pinch of salt

Vanilla ice cream for serving

» AN ICING SPATULA or a knife with a long, straight edge is the best tool for applying frosting in clean, ripple-free sweeps.

FLOWER GARDEN NAKED CAKE

A naked cake isn't exactly naked, just barely frosted on the sides so that each layer of cake is still visible. Decorate the top with a colorful arrangement of fresh edible flowers, such as rose petals, violets, clover, pansies, or nasturtiums.

1 PREPARE THE CAKE PANS

Preheat the oven to 350°F. Grease three 8-inch round cake pans, line the bottoms of the pans with parchment paper, then grease the parchment. Dust with flour, then tap out any excess.

2 MAKE THE BATTER

In a small bowl, stir together the flour, baking powder, and salt. Set aside. In a large bowl, using an electric mixer, beat the butter, sugar, and vanilla on medium speed until creamy, about 3 minutes. Add the eggs one at a time, beating well after each addition. With the mixer on low speed, beat in the flour mixture in 3 additions, alternating with the milk in 2 additions.

3 BAKE THE CAKE

Divide the batter between the prepared pans. Bake until a toothpick inserted into the center of each cake comes out clean, 30–35 minutes. Let cool in the pans on wire racks for 5 minutes. Remove the cakes from the pans and let cool on the racks.

4 DECORATE THE CAKE

Evenly slice off a thin layer from the rounded top of each cake to make it level, if necessary. Place a cake layer on a serving plate. Top with 1 cup buttercream, spreading it evenly. Place a second cake layer over the buttercream and spread another 1 cup buttercream on top. Place the third cake layer, bottom side up, on top. Using an offset icing spatula or other straight-edged knife, spread the remaining buttercream over the top and in a single sheer layer over the cake sides so that each layer is still visible. Garnish the top with edible blossoms, cut the cake into wedges, and serve.

¾ cup unsalted butter, at room temperature, plus butter for greasing

2¼ cups all-purpose flour, plus flour for dusting

1 tablespoon baking powder

¼ teaspoon salt

1¾ cups sugar

2 teaspoons pure vanilla extract

3 large eggs, at room temperature

1⅓ cups milk, at room temperature

3 cups Vanilla Buttercream (page 125)

Edible flowers for garnish

LEMON MERINGUE PIE

The secrets to lemon meringue pie success include adding the hot lemon filling to the fully baked crust, immediately topping the filling with the meringue, and spreading the meringue so that it conceals the filling completely. For a shortcut, use a store-bought pie shell instead of one that's homemade.

1 MAKE THE PIE PASTRY SHELL

Make the pie pastry and parbake the pie shell as directed. Let cool.

2 MAKE THE LEMON CUSTARD

In a small bowl, stir together the cornstarch and ½ cup of the water until the cornstarch dissolves. In a saucepan, whisk together the egg yolks, sugar, lemon juice, and remaining 1 cup water until well blended. Whisk in the cornstarch mixture and bring to a boil over medium heat while whisking constantly, about 8 minutes. Boil until the mixture thickens and looks almost translucent, about 1 minute. Remove the pan from the heat and stir in the lemon zest. Immediately pour the hot filling into the cooled crust.

3 MAKE THE MERINGUE

Preheat the broiler. Arrange the rack about 8 inches from the heat source. In a bowl, combine the egg whites and cream of tartar. Beat with an electric mixer on medium speed until foamy, about 2 minutes. Raise the speed to medium-high and slowly add the sugar. Beat until shiny, soft peaks form, about 3 minutes.

4 ASSEMBLE THE PIE

Spread the meringue over the warm filling so that it completely covers the pie, mounding it toward the center and spreading it out to the edges to completely seal the filling inside the crust without any gaps. Use the back of a spoon to form swirls and peaks on the meringue. Broil until the meringue is lightly browned, about 5 minutes. Transfer the pie to a wire rack and let cool for 1 hour, then refrigerate for at least 2 hours or up to overnight before serving.

1 homemade Pie Pastry Shell (page 104), or 1 purchased pie pastry in 9-inch pan, parbaked according to package directions

FOR THE LEMON CUSTARD
6 tablespoons cornstarch
1½ cups water
5 large egg yolks
1¾ cups sugar
½ cup fresh lemon juice
2 teaspoons grated lemon zest

FOR THE MERINGUE
5 large egg whites
¼ teaspoon cream of tartar
½ cup sugar

FRENCH APPLE TART

Purchased or homemade pie pastry makes an easy, crisp shell for tender apple slices. To make a traditional tart shell, which is lighter and more crumbly than a pie crust, follow the recipe for Pie Pastry (page 104) through step 1, adding one beaten egg with the water and reducing the amount of water to two tablespoons.

1 LINE THE TART PAN

On a lightly floured work surface, roll out the dough into a 12-inch round. Drape the dough over a rolling pin and transfer it to a 9-inch tart pan with a removable bottom. Gently slip the dough from the pin and press it into the pan. Using a knife or kitchen scissors, trim the pastry edge about 1 inch beyond the pan rim. Fold the pastry edge in to make the folded edge even with the pan rim, then press the dough firmly against the pan rim. Refrigerate the pastry-lined pan in the refrigerator for 30 minutes. Preheat the oven to 375°F.

2 PARBAKE THE TART SHELL

Parbake the tart shell as directed on page 104, step 3. Let cool.

3 ADD THE FILLING

Peel the apples, cut in half, and remove the cores. Place the apple halves, cut side down, on a cutting board and cut lengthwise into thin slices. (Alternatively, use a rotary peeler to core, peel, and slice the apples at the same time.) Spread the apple sauce evenly over the bottom of the shell. Arrange the apple slices on top of the sauce in concentric circles. Brush the apple slices with the melted butter, coating them evenly, then sprinkle with the sugar.

4 BAKE THE TART

Bake until golden, about 50 minutes. Remove the pan from the oven. Using a pastry brush, brush the jelly mixture evenly over the apple slices. Let cool. Remove the pan sides and transfer the tart to a serving plate. Cut into wedges and serve.

All-purpose flour for dusting

Purchased or homemade Pie Pastry Shell (page 104) through step 1, or tart dough (see note)

2 tart green apples, such as Granny Smith or pippin

1 snack-size container (about 4 oz) unsweetened apple sauce

2 tablespoons unsalted butter, melted

1 tablespoon sugar

1 tablespoon apple jelly mixed with 1 teaspoon water

PIE PASTRY SHELL

To ensure a flaky crust, keep the butter cold and don't overwork the dough.
You should see small chunks of butter in the finished dough.

1 MAKE THE PIE PASTRY

In a bowl, mix the flour, sugar, and salt. Scatter the butter over the
flour mixture. With a pastry blender, 2 knives, or your fingertips, cut
the butter into the flour mixture until large, coarse crumbs form.
Sprinkle in the water 1 tablespoon at a time, stirring and tossing
with a fork after each addition until the dough comes together in a
rough, shaggy mass. Dump out the dough onto a piece of plastic
wrap, cover with the wrap, and shape into a flat disk. Refrigerate
for at least 30 minutes or up to overnight.

2 LINE A PIE DISH

Unwrap the dough, place on a lightly floured work surface, and dust
with flour. Using a rolling pin, roll out the dough into a 12-inch round,
lifting and turning the dough and dusting the work surface with
flour as needed. Roll the dough loosely around the rolling pin and
unroll it over the center of 9-inch pie pan or dish. Gently press
the dough into the bottom and up the sides of the pan or dish.
Using kitchen scissors or a knife, trim away the rough edge of the
dough, leaving a 1-inch overhang. Fold the dough overhang under to
create an even rim, then finish the pie rim with a decorative edge:
Use the tines of a fork to crimp the dough rim, or use your fingers
to pinch the dough rim into a scalloped edge. Place the dough-lined
pie pan into the refrigerator until firm, about 30 minutes.

3 PARBAKE THE PIE SHELL

Preheat the oven to 375°F. Line the crust with aluminum foil and
fill it with pie weights or dried beans to prevent the pastry from
buckling in the heat of the oven. Bake for 20 minutes, remove the
weights and foil, then continue baking until pale gold, about
5 minutes longer. Transfer to a wire rack and let cool.

1½ cups all-purpose flour

1 tablespoon sugar, optional

½ teaspoon salt

½ cup cold, unsalted butter,
cut into tablespoon-size pieces

4-5 tablespoons ice cold water,
plus more as needed

HOW TO MAKE PIE PASTRY

1

Cut the butter into the flour mixture until large, coarse crumbs form.

2

Gradually sprinkle in the ice water, mixing with a fork to form a rough, shaggy mass.

3

Dump out the dough from the bowl onto a piece of plastic wrap.

4

Cover the dough with the plastic wrap, shape into a disk, and refrigerate for 30 minutes.

5

Roll out the dough on a lightly floured work surface until about ⅛-inch thick.

6

Loosely roll the dough onto the rolling pin, then unroll it over a 9-inch pie pan or dish.

7

Gently press the dough into the bottom and pan sides.

8

Cut around the rim, leaving a 1-inch overhang.

9

Fold the overhang under to create an even rim, then decoratively flute the edge.

DOUBLE BERRY GALETTE

This free-form tart is an easy way to showcase ripe, seasonal berries. You can try the same method with sliced apples or peaches for equally delicious results. If you're pressed for time, swap in store-bought pie dough for the homemade.

1 PREPARE THE PAN
Preheat the oven to 425°F. Line a rimmed baking sheet with parchment paper.

2 ROLL OUT THE DOUGH
On a lightly floured work surface, roll out the dough into a round 11–12 inches in diameter and about ⅛ inch thick. Transfer to the prepared sheet.

3 MAKE THE GALETTE
In a bowl, toss together the berries, lemon juice, granulated sugar, and flour. Spoon the filling onto the dough, leaving a 2-inch border uncovered around the edge. Fold the edge up and over the filling, forming loose pleats. Brush the border with the egg wash and sprinkle with the turbinado sugar, if using.

4 BAKE & SERVE THE GALETTE
Bake until the filling is bubbling and the pastry is golden brown, about 25 minutes. Let cool slightly on a wire rack. Cut into wedges and serve topped with whipped cream.

Purchased or homemade
Pie Pastry Shell (page 104)
through step 1

2 cups blackberries

2 cups blueberries

2 tablespoons fresh lemon juice

¼ cup granulated sugar

3 tablespoons all-purpose flour

1 large egg beaten with
1 teaspoon water (optional)

1 tablespoon turbinado sugar
(optional)

Whipped cream for serving

» TURBINADO SUGAR, sprinkled over the dough edge just before baking, ensures a sweet, caramelized, and crispy exterior to the baked crust.

NO-BAKE CHEESECAKE JARS

These single-serving cheesecake treats are easy and delicious. Use a spoon to dig down to the graham cracker base, blending a bit of the crumbly crust, creamy middle, and fruity top in each bite.

1 MAKE THE CRUST

In a small bowl, combine the graham cracker crumbs, butter, and 2 tablespoons sugar until blended. Divide the mixture among five 8-oz jars or glasses, then use the blunt bottom end of a kitchen knife or wooden spoon to tamp down the crumbs. Refrigerate until firm, 10–15 minutes.

2 MAKE THE CREAM FILLING

Meanwhile, in a large bowl, beat the cream cheese and remaining ⅓ cup sugar with an electric mixer on medium speed or by hand until smooth. Beat in ¼ cup of the cream, the lemon juice, and the vanilla.

3 FILL THE JARS

Put the water in a microwave-safe cup. Sprinkle the gelatin over the water and let soften for 2 minutes. Microwave on high until the gelatin dissolves, about 5 seconds. Stir in the remaining ¼ cup cream. Add the gelatin mixture to the cream cheese mixture and beat until fluffy, about 1 minute with an electric mixer on medium speed or 3 minutes by hand. Spoon the filling into the jars, dividing it evenly. Cover and refrigerate until firm, at least 1 hour or up to 2 days. Divide the fruit evenly among the jars before serving.

¾ cup graham cracker crumbs (from about 6 graham crackers)

2 tablespoons unsalted butter, at room temperature

2 tablespoons plus ⅓ cup sugar

1 lb cream cheese, at room temperature

½ cup heavy cream

1 tablespoon fresh lemon juice

½ teaspoon pure vanilla extract

1 tablespoon water

½ teaspoon unflavored gelatin

1 cup fresh berries, halved pitted fresh cherries, or diced fresh peaches, mangoes, or kiwis

RASPBERRY MACARONS

Perfect French macarons—delicately crisp on the outside, featherlight and a tad chewy on the inside—are the test of a true baker. To make piping easy and precise, use a math compass, small glass, or other circular guide to draw evenly spaced circles on each piece of parchment to help guide you.

1 PREPARE THE BAKING SHEETS

Line 2 baking sheets with parchment paper.

2 COMBINE THE NUTS AND SUGAR

Combine the almond flour and 1 cup of the powdered sugar in a sifter or fine-mesh sieve. Set aside.

3 BEAT THE EGG WHITES

In a bowl, using an electric mixer, beat the egg whites, vanilla and almond extracts, and salt on medium speed until soft peaks form, about 3 minutes. Increase the speed to high and gradually beat in the remaining 1 cup powdered sugar, beating until stiff peaks form. Beat in the food coloring until the desired shade of pink is reached.

4 FOLD IN THE NUT MIXTURE

Sift about one-quarter of the almond-sugar mixture over the beaten whites. Using a silicone spatula, fold it in until blended. Repeat to fold in the remaining almond-sugar mixture, one-quarter at a time, until incorporated and the batter flows like lava.

5 FILL THE PIPING BAG

Place a pastry bag fitted with a ⅜-inch round tip (or a plastic bag with a ⅜-inch hole snipped in a corner) tip-end down in a glass. Fold back the open end of the bag over the sides of the glass to hold it open. Spoon the batter into the bag and secure closed.

Continued on page 112 »

1⅓ cup superfine almond flour

2 cups powdered sugar

3 large egg whites

½ teaspoon pure vanilla extract

½ teaspoon almond extract

Pinch of salt

3 drops rose-pink gel paste food coloring, plus more if needed

About ½ cup seedless raspberry jam

HOW TO MAKE MACARONS

1

Hold a cracked egg over a bowl. Pass the yolk from one half to the other, letting the white fall into the bowl.

2

Set the yolks aside for another use. Beat the whites to soft peaks.

3

Gradually beat the powdered sugar into the egg whites.

4

Continue to beat the egg whites until stiff peaks form.

5

Fold in the nuts by running the spatula from underneath the mixture to over the top.

6

Fold the open end of a pastry bag over a glass rim. Fill the bag with the egg white mixture.

7

To pipe the same size cookies, use a glass or compass to draw circles on parchment paper.

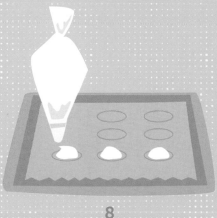

8

Place the paper circle-side down on a baking sheet. Pipe the meringues on top.

9

Spoon jam onto the flat sides of half of the cookies, then sandwich with the remaining halves.

» Continued from page 110

6 **PIPE THE BATTER**

Holding the piping bag upright and with the tip about ½ inch above a prepared baking sheet, pipe about 25 1½–1¾ inch mounds of batter onto each sheet, piping even mounds spaced about 1 inch apart; make the mounds as smooth as possible, moving the bag off to one side after each mound is piped. Tap each sheet firmly against the work surface 2 or 3 times to release any air bubbles.

7 **BAKE THE COOKIES**

Place the rack in the lower third of the oven and preheat the oven to 325°F. Let the cookies stand at room temperature for 30–45 minutes. Bake 1 baking sheet at a time, rotating the pan halfway through baking, until risen and just set (but not browned), 10–11 minutes. The bottom of the cookies should be dry and firm to the touch. Transfer the cookies to a wire rack and let cool completely.

8 **SANDWICH THE COOKIES**

Spoon about ½ teaspoon jam over the flat side of half of the cookies. Top them with the remaining cookies, flat side down. Place the cookies in a single layer on a baking sheet, cover with plastic wrap, and refrigerate for at least 1 day or up to 3 days, or freeze for up to 6 months. (If frozen, thaw in the refrigerator before serving.) Serve chilled or at cool room temperature.

FRESH MINT ICE CREAM WITH SHAVED CHOCOLATE

For the best chocolate-shaving technique, use a vegetable peeler or sharp knife to cut flat, thin shavings from a room-temperature block of chocolate.

1 MAKE THE CUSTARD

In a heavy saucepan, combine the cream, milk, and mint leaves. Warm over medium-high heat, stirring occasionally, until the mixture barely comes to a simmer, about 5 minutes. Meanwhile, in a heatproof bowl, combine the egg yolks, sugar, and salt. Whisk vigorously until the mixture lightens in color and doubles in volume, about 2 minutes. Remove the cream mixture from the heat. Whisking constantly, slowly pour about 1 cup of the warm cream mixture into the egg mixture, then whisk the combined mixture back into the saucepan and place over medium heat. Using a wooden spoon, stir until the mixture forms a custard thick enough to coat the back of the spoon, 1–2 minutes; do not boil.

2 CHILL THE CUSTARD

Set up an ice bath in a large bowl and nestle a smaller bowl inside. Pour the custard through a fine-mesh sieve into the smaller bowl; stir occasionally until cool. Remove the bowl from the ice bath, stir in the food coloring (if using), and cover with plastic wrap. Refrigerate until very cold, at least 4 hours or up to 3 days.

3 CHURN THE ICE CREAM

Pour the cold custard into an ice cream maker and churn according to the manufacturer's instructions. Add the shaved chocolate during the last minute of churning. Spoon the ice cream into a freezer-safe container and place a sheet of parchment or waxed paper directly on the surface. Cover tightly and freeze until firm, at least 2 hours or up to 3 days.

1¾ cups heavy cream

1½ cups whole milk

¾ cup fresh mint leaves

4 large egg yolks

¾ cup sugar

⅛ teaspoon salt

2 drops green food coloring (optional)

4 oz bittersweet chocolate, shaved (see note) or finely chopped

SEMISWEET CHOCOLATE CUPS

These delicious cups spiff up even the simplest dessert. Fill them with Chocolate Mousse (page 120), Fresh Mint Ice Cream (page 113), or whipped cream and berries. Small four-inch balloons, like those used for water balloons, are the best size for making them.

1 MELT THE CHOCOLATE

In a microwave-safe bowl, combine the chocolate chips and shortening. Microwave on high power, stirring every 20 seconds, just until the mixture is melted and smooth. Let the mixture cool until barely warm, 10–15 minutes. Meanwhile, blow up 6 small balloons and knot each one at the end. Line a rimmed baking sheet with waxed paper.

2 MAKE THE CUPS

When the chocolate has cooled, hold a balloon by the knotted end and dip it into the melted chocolate, covering about 3 inches of the balloon bottom. Place the chocolate-dipped balloon, chocolate side down, on the prepared baking sheet. Repeat to dip the remaining balloons, placing them on the baking sheet. When all the balloons are dipped, place the baking sheet in the refrigerator until the chocolate is set, 5–10 minutes. When the chocolate is set, pop the balloons with a pin and discard them. Set the bowls aside at cool room temperature until ready to use, or refrigerate for up to 1 day.

1 cup semisweet or
bittersweet chocolate chips

**1 tablespoon solid
vegetable shortening**

6 small balloons

1 Melt the chocolate in a bowl set over a saucepan.

2 Dip the small balloons into the melted chocolate.

3 Once set, pop the balloons in the cups and remove.

SALTED CHOCOLATE CHUNK COOKIES

Flaky shards of sea salt add unexpected crunch and a hit of flavor to these generously sized cookies. If you prefer your cookies plain, skip the flaky salt. Store the cookies in an airtight container at room temperature for up to 5 days.

1 PREPARE THE BAKING SHEETS

Preheat the oven to 350°F. Line 2 baking sheets with parchment paper.

2 MAKE THE DOUGH

In a bowl, whisk together the flour, baking soda, and salt. Set aside. In a large bowl, beat the butter, brown sugar, and granulated sugar with an electric mixer on low speed or by hand until combined, then beat on medium speed or briskly by hand until light and fluffy, about 3 minutes. Add the eggs one at a time, beating well after each addition. Add the vanilla and beat to combine. Gradually beat in the flour mixture on low speed or by hand, beating just until combined. Stir in the chocolate chunks until evenly combined.

3 BAKE THE COOKIES

Spoon nine 1½- to 2-inch balls of dough onto each prepared baking sheet, placing them at least 2 inches apart. Sprinkle the cookies evenly with sea salt. Bake until lightly browned, 12–15 minutes. Let the cookies cool on the baking sheets for 5 minutes, then transfer to wire racks to cool completely.

3 ¾ cups all-purpose flour

1¼ teaspoons baking soda

1 teaspoon salt

1¼ cups unsalted butter, at room temperature

1 cup firmly packed golden brown sugar

¾ cup granulated sugar

3 large eggs

2 teaspoons pure vanilla extract

1 bag (10 – 11½ oz) large chocolate chunks

Flaky sea salt for sprinkling

APRICOT SWIRL COOKIES

Once rolled and wrapped in waxed paper, these rolls can be refrigerated for up to 1 week or frozen for up to 3 months. Let thaw before cutting and baking.

1 MAKE THE FILLING

In a small saucepan, combine the apricots, orange juice, and water. Bring to a boil over medium-high heat, reduce the heat to medium-low, and simmer, until 2 tablespoons liquid remains, about 5 minutes. Transfer to a food processor and purée until smooth. Let cool.

2 MAKE THE DOUGH

Meanwhile, in a large bowl, using an electric mixer (preferably with a paddle attachment), beat the butter, sugar, and vanilla on medium-high speed until light and creamy, about 2 minutes. Beat in the flour on low speed until blended and smooth.

3 ROLL & REFRIGERATE THE DOUGH

Place an 8-inch piece of waxed paper on a work surface. Transfer half of the dough to the waxed paper and dust lightly with flour. Using a lightly floured rolling pin, roll out the dough into a 6 x 6-inch square, pressing the dough with your hands to define the shape. Spread half of the apricot purée evenly over the square. Starting at one end, lift up the waxed paper to help you roll up the dough into a log, enclosing the purée inside. Refrigerate the roll until well chilled, about 30 minutes. Repeat with the remaining dough.

4 CUT THE DOUGH

Preheat the oven to 350°F. Line 2 baking sheets with parchment paper. Remove the rolls from the waxed paper. Place each roll, seam side down, on a cutting board. Using a serrated knife, carefully cut each log crosswise in half, then cut each half into 8 slices, wiping the knife blade on a paper towel between slices.

5 BAKE THE COOKIES

Transfer the slices to the prepared baking sheets. Bake until just golden at the edges, 12–14 minutes. Let cool briefly, then serve.

1 cup (about 5½ oz) dried apricots

¾ cup orange juice

¼ cup water

¾ cup unsalted butter, at room temperature

¾ cup powdered sugar

1 teaspoon pure vanilla extract

1½ cups all-purpose flour, plus flour for dusting

CARAMEL SAUCE is a tasty partner for bananas, but you can always use chocolate sauce instead.

CRISP BANANA SPRING ROLLS WITH CARAMEL SAUCE

This delicious dessert comes together in minutes. To make it even quicker, swap in purchased caramel sauce for the homemade.

Canola oil for frying

4 bananas

16 egg roll wrappers

16 **teaspoons** firmly packed golden brown sugar

Ground cinnamon for sprinkling

Vanilla ice cream for serving

1 cup Caramel Sauce (page 125) for serving

1 HEAT THE OIL

In a large, deep sauté pan, heat about 1 inch of oil over medium heat until it reaches 375°F on a deep-frying thermometer or until a small piece of an egg roll wrapper dropped into the oil begins to brown in about 20 seconds.

2 PREPARE THE SPRING ROLLS

Cut the bananas in half lengthwise, then in half again crosswise. Set aside a small bowl of water. Work with one egg roll wrapper at a time, keeping the remaining wrappers covered with a kitchen towel to prevent drying. Lay an egg roll wrapper on a work surface with one corner pointing toward you. Place a banana piece on the bottom third of the wrapper. Sprinkle with 1 teaspoon brown sugar, then dust with cinnamon. Fold the bottom corner over the banana, fold in the side corners, then roll up the banana in the wrapper. Moisten the top corner with a dab of water, then press the corner against the roll to seal it shut. Set aside. Repeat to make all the rolls.

3 FRY THE ROLLS

Working in batches, use a slotted spoon to lower 3 or 4 spring rolls at a time into the hot oil. Fry, turning if needed, until crisp and evenly browned, about 1 minute. Using the slotted spoon, transfer the rolls to a plate lined with paper towels to drain. Let cool briefly.

4 SERVE THE SPRING ROLLS

Scoop ice cream into 8 small bowls. Place 2 spring rolls in each bowl. Drizzle some of the caramel sauce over the ice cream and rolls and serve, passing the remaining caramel sauce at the table.

CHOCOLATE MOUSSE IN CHOCOLATE CUPS

Chocolate mousse is all about technique. Be sure to melt the chocolate gently, whip the cream firmly, then fold it all together with a light hand. The chocolate cups are an extra step but worth the effort. For a shortcut, simply spoon the chocolate mousse into small serving cups instead.

1 MELT THE CHOCOLATE

Pour about 1 inch of water into a small saucepan and bring to a simmer over medium-low heat. Put the chopped chocolate in a heatproof bowl that is slightly larger than the saucepan and place it on the saucepan, making sure that the bowl does not touch the simmering water below. Heat, stirring often, until melted and smooth, about 5 minutes. Let cool. (To speed cooling, nestle the bowl of chocolate in a large bowl filled with ice-cold water and stir until the chocolate is room temperature.)

2 MAKE THE MOUSSE

In a bowl, combine the cream, powdered sugar, and vanilla. Beat with an electric mixer on medium-high speed until firm peaks form. Scoop about one-third of the whipped cream on top of the cooled chocolate and whisk until blended and smooth. Using a silicone spatula, gently fold the remaining whipped cream into the chocolate mixture just until combined. Use a light hand so you don't deflate the cream.

3 SERVE THE MOUSSE

Spoon the mousse into the chocolate cups. Cover and refrigerate for at least 2 hours or up to overnight. If desired, spoon a small dollop of whipped cream and a sprinkling of fresh strawberries into each cup before serving.

10 oz semisweet or bittersweet chocolate, finely chopped

1½ cups heavy cream, chilled

⅔ cup powdered sugar

1 teaspoon pure vanilla extract

6 Semisweet Chocolate Cups (page 114) for serving

Lightly whipped cream for serving (optional)

6 strawberries, sliced (optional)

SWEET-AND-SPICY CHAI MILKSHAKES

Chai is the word for "tea" in India, and it is often brewed with sweetened hot milk and a mixture of warm, aromatic spices. Black peppercorns might seem like an unusual addition to a sweet drink, but their flavor goes really well with the other spices in the mix.

1 INFUSE THE MILK WITH SPICES

Combine the milk and sugar in a saucepan. Set the pan over medium-high heat and heat the milk, stirring to dissolve the sugar, until steam begins to rise. Remove from the heat and add the tea bags, peppercorns, and ginger. Steep for 5 minutes, then remove the tea bags. Let cool.

2 CHILL THE SPICED MILK

Transfer the mixture to a container, cover, and refrigerate until cold, at least 2 hours or up to overnight. (To chill the chai quickly, transfer it from the saucepan to a bowl and nestle it in a larger bowl filled with ice.)

3 BLEND THE MILKSHAKE

Set a fine-mesh sieve over the top of a blender and strain the chai into the blender. Add the ice cream and blend until smooth. Divide the milkshake evenly among 4 glasses. If desired, top with dollops of whipped cream and sprinkle with cinnamon, then serve.

4 cups whole milk

2 tablespoons sugar

4 chai tea bags

10 black peppercorns

3 thin slices peeled fresh ginger

1 pint vanilla ice cream, slightly softened

Whipped cream for serving (optional)

Ground cinnamon for serving (optional)

BASIC RECIPES

COOKED CHICKEN

Makes 1–2 servings

1–2 boneless, skinless chicken breasts
¼–½ teaspoon salt
¼ teaspoon black peppercorns
1 clove garlic, smashed
4 fresh herb sprigs, such as thyme or parsley

Put the chicken in a single layer in a saucepan. Add water to cover by 1–2 inches. Add the salt, peppercorns, garlic, and herbs. Bring to a boil over medium-high heat, then immediately reduce the heat to low, cover, and simmer until the chicken is opaque throughout, 10–14 minutes. Transfer the chicken to a cutting board and let cool, then use as directed, or refrigerate in an airtight container for up to 3 days.

BASIC PORK BRINE

Makes 6½ cups

6 cups water
¼ cup cider vinegar
¼ cup firmly packed golden brown sugar
2 tablespoons kosher salt
1 teaspoon freshly ground black pepper
1 teaspoon dried thyme
1 teaspoon juniper berries (optional)
⅛ teaspoon red pepper flakes

In a large bowl, combine all the ingredients. Stir until the sugar and salt dissolve. Use as directed.

ADOBO MARINADE

Makes about ½ cup

1 canned chipotle pepper in adobo, plus 1 tablespoon adobo sauce
¼ yellow onion
1 clove garlic
2 tablespoons olive oil
½ teaspoon ground cumin
½ teaspoon dried oregano
Kosher salt and freshly ground pepper

In a food processor, combine the chipotle and adobo sauce, onion, garlic, olive oil, cumin, oregano, ½ teaspoon salt, and a few grinds of pepper. Process until smooth, scraping down the sides of the bowl as needed. Use at once, or transfer to an airtight container, cover, and refrigerate for up to 3 days.

CROUTONS

Makes about 1 cup

2 tablespoons unsalted butter
2 tablespoons olive oil
2 slices sourdough bread, cut or torn into ½ x 1½-inch pieces (about 1 cup)
Salt and freshly ground pepper

In a large frying pan, heat the butter and oil over medium heat. When the butter has melted, add the bread pieces and cook, stirring occasionally, until crisp and golden brown, about 5 minutes.

Season to taste with salt and pepper. Remove from the heat and set aside until ready to use, or store in an airtight container at room temperature for up to 3 days.

STEAMED WHITE RICE

Makes 3 cups

1 cup long-grain white rice, such as jasmine or basmati

1½ cups water

¼ teaspoon salt

In a saucepan, bring the rice, water, and salt to a boil over high heat. Reduce the heat to low, give the rice a stir, cover, and cook, without lifting the lid, until the liquid is absorbed and the rice is tender, about 20 minutes. Remove from the heat and let stand, covered, for 10 minutes. Uncover, fluff with a fork, and serve.

STEAMED BROWN RICE

Makes 3 cups

1 cup short-grain brown rice

2 cups water

¼ teaspoon salt

In a saucepan, bring the rice, water, and salt to a boil over high heat. Reduce the heat to low, give the rice a stir, cover, and cook, without lifting the lid, until the liquid is absorbed and the rice is tender, 45–50 minutes. Remove from the heat and let stand, covered, for 10 minutes. Uncover, fluff with a fork, and serve.

COCONUT–GREEN ONION RICE

Makes 3 cups

2 teaspoons canola oil

1 green onion, thinly sliced

½ teaspoon minced, peeled ginger

1 cup jasmine rice

1 cup water

½ cup coconut milk

½ teaspoon kosher salt

¼ cup shredded coconut, toasted (optional)

In a saucepan, heat the canola oil over medium-high heat. Add the green onion and ginger and cook until fragrant, about 30 seconds. Add the rice and stir to mix. Add the water, coconut milk, and salt and bring to a boil. Reduce the heat to low, cover, and simmer until the liquid is absorbed and the rice is tender, about 20 minutes. Remove from the heat and let stand, covered, for 10 minutes. Uncover, fluff with a fork, stir in the coconut (if using), and serve.

STEAMED QUINOA

Makes 3 cups

1 cup quinoa, rinsed

2 cups water or reduced-sodium chicken broth

½ teaspoon salt

In a saucepan, bring the quinoa, water, and salt to a boil over high heat. Reduce the heat to low, give the quinoa a stir, cover, and cook, without lifting the lid, until the liquid is absorbed and the quinoa is tender, about 15 minutes. Remove from the heat and let stand, covered, for 5 minutes. Uncover, fluff with a fork, and serve.

SALSA VERDE

Makes about ⅔ cup

2 large cloves garlic, minced
¼ teaspoon salt
3 tablespoons olive oil
1 tablespoon fresh lime juice
¼ bunch fresh flat-leaf parsley, minced
¼ bunch fresh cilantro, minced
½ teaspoon freshly ground black pepper
¼ teaspoon red pepper flakes

In a small bowl, use the back of a spoon to mash the garlic with the salt until a paste forms. Stir in the oil, lime juice, parsley, cilantro, black pepper, and red pepper flakes. Use at once, or transfer to an airtight container, top with a thin layer of oil, cover, and refrigerate for up to 1 week.

FRESH BASIL PESTO

Makes about 1 cup

1 or 2 cloves garlic
¼ cup pine nuts
2 cups packed fresh basil leaves
½ cup extra-virgin olive oil
½ cup freshly grated Parmesan cheese
Salt and freshly ground pepper

With a food processor running, drop the garlic through the feed tube and process until minced. Turn off the processor, add the pine nuts, and pulse a few times to chop. Add the basil and pulse a few times to chop coarsely. Then, with the processor running, add the oil through the feed tube in a slow, steady stream and process until a smooth, moderately thick paste forms, stopping to scrape down the bowl as needed. Transfer to a bowl and stir in the Parmesan. Season to taste with salt and pepper. Use at once, or transfer to an airtight container, top with a thin layer of oil, cover, and refrigerate for up to 1 week.

YOGURT SAUCE

Makes about 1 cup

¾ cup plain whole-milk yogurt
Grated zest and juice of 1 lemon
1 tablespoon chopped fresh cilantro
1–2 tablespoons water
Salt and freshly ground pepper

In a small bowl, stir together the yogurt, lemon zest and juice, and cilantro. Stir in the water, a little at a time, until the sauce has a good, pourable consistency. Season to taste with salt and pepper. Use at once, or store in an airtight container in the refrigerator for up to 2 days.

TZATZIKI

Makes about 2 cups

1 cup plain whole-milk regular or Greek yogurt
1 cup peeled and grated English cucumber
1 teaspoon minced fresh mint or flat-leaf parsley
1 teaspoon fresh lemon juice
Salt

In a bowl, combine the yogurt, cucumber, mint or parsley, and lemon juice and stir until well combined. Season to taste with salt. Use at once, or transfer to an airtight container and store in the refrigerator for up to 2 days.

NECTARINE SALSA

Makes about 1½ cups

3 nectarines, pitted and cut into wedges
1 tablespoon fresh lime juice
2 teaspoons seeded and minced jalapeño chile
2 tablespoons chopped fresh cilantro
2 tablespoons chopped red onion

In a bowl, combine the nectarines, lime juice, jalapeno, cilantro, and red onion. Toss to mix.

VANILLA BUTTERCREAM

Makes about 3 cups

2 cups unsalted butter, at room temperature
3 cups powdered sugar
2 teaspoons pure vanilla extract
⅛ teaspoon kosher salt

In the bowl of a stand mixer fitted with the paddle attachment, beat the butter on medium speed until smooth, about 2 minutes. Add the sugar, vanilla, and salt, increase the speed to medium-high, and beat until combined, stopping the mixer to scrape down the sides of the bowl as needed. Use at once, or store in an airtight container at room temperature for up to 1 day.

APPLE SYRUP

Makes about 1⅓ cups

1 cup apple juice
1 cup pure maple syrup

In a small saucepan, bring the apple juice to a boil over high heat. Boil until reduced to about ⅓ cup, about 10 minutes. Remove from the heat and whisk in the maple syrup. Keep warm for serving.

CARAMEL SAUCE

Makes about 2 cups

1 cup sugar
¼ cup water
⅔ cup heavy cream
2 tablespoons unsalted butter

In a sauté pan, off the heat, combine the sugar and water and stir, being careful not to splash the mixture up the sides of the pan. Place the pan over medium-high heat and stir gently until the sugar begins to dissolve, about 30 seconds. Stop stirring and cook until the mixture turns a deep golden color, about 5 minutes. If it begins to brown unevenly, give the pan a quick swirl or stir the mixture. (Be careful because the mixture will be very hot and sticky!) When the caramel turns a deep golden brown, remove the pan from the heat and carefully and slowly pour in the cream, whisking rapidly. (There will be lots of steam and bubbling!) Continue whisking rapidly until all the cream is incorporated. Add the butter and stir until dissolved. Let cool. Use at once, or store in an airtight container in the refrigerator for up to 2 weeks.

VANILLA DOUGHNUT GLAZE

Makes about 3 cups

6 tablespoons unsalted butter, melted
2½ cups powdered sugar
5 tablespoons hot water, plus more as needed
1 teaspoon pure vanilla extract

In a bowl, whisk together the melted butter, sugar, hot water, and vanilla until smooth. Whisk in 1–2 teaspoons more hot water if needed to give the glaze a good consistency. Use as directed.

INDEX

JUNIOR CHEF MASTER CLASS COOKBOOK

Conceived and produced by Weldon Owen International
in collaboration with Williams Sonoma, Inc.
3250 Van Ness Avenue, San Francisco, CA 94109

Printed in the China
First printed in 2019
10 9 8 7 6 5 4 3

Library of Congress Cataloging-in-Publication
data is available.

ISBN: 978-1-68188-474-5

WELDON OWEN INTERNATIONAL
President & Publisher Roger Shaw
SVP, Sales & Marketing Amy Kaneko
Associate Publisher Amy Marr
Senior Editor Lisa Atwood
Creative Director Kelly Booth
Art Director Meghan Hildebrand
Imaging Manager Don Hill

Photographer Aubrie Pick
Food Stylist Karen Shinto
Prop Stylist Claire Mack
Illustration Marisa Kwek

1150 Brickyard Cove Road
Richmond, CA 94801
www.weldonowen.com

ACKNOWLEDGMENTS

Weldon Owen wishes to thank the following people for their generous support
in producing this book: Lisa Berman, Lesley Bruynesteyn, Josephine Hsu,
Bessma Khalaf, Kim Laidlaw, Mary Lee, Ashley Lima, Elizabeth Parson, and Karen Wise.